INTEGRATING COMPUTERS IN YOUR CLASSROOM

MIDDLE AND SECONDARY MATH

BY PETER DUBLIN, HARVEY PRESSMAN,

WILLIAM JOHNSON and BEV A. MAWN

HarperCollins*College*Publishers

This book was developed and produced by Intentional Educations, Inc. of Watertown, Massachusetts. Intentional Educations is one of the country's foremost developers of educational materials, both books and software. We wish to thank the following people for their contribution to this book:

Interior book design:
    Dee Nee Reiten-Skipper
Cover design and mechanicals:
    Sylvia Frezzolini
Cover illustrations:
    Marti Shohet
Interior cartoons:
    Larry Butler
Part I interior illustrations:
    Cheryl Kirk Noll
Part II interior illustrations:
    Elizabeth Manicatide
Editorial assistance:
    Susan Christie Woodward
    Andrea Infantino
    Melissa Willson
Typesetting:
    Peter Dublin

ISBN: 0-06-501678-5

94 95 96 97 9 8 7 6 5 4 3 2 1

Contents

PREFACE

The computer will play an important part in schools if it plays an important part in classrooms. The classroom remains the cornerstone of education in schools, so for computers to be important in schools, they must be important in classrooms. That is the reason this book is entitled "Integrating Computers in Your Classroom." That is the reason we make precious little mention of Computer Labs or Media Centers.

Computers have been knocking on the doors of education for over thirty years. Through the 1970's, time-sharing, mainframes, and programmed instruction dominated computer activity in the schools. From the end of the 1970's through the 1980's, the personal computer led the so-called "computer revolution" in the schools. Now, in the 1990's, many are wondering whether this "revolution" might have passed us by.

We believe the fundamental changes in education are still ahead of us, and that computers can play an important role in helping to shape those changes. The changes, however are not likely to be primarily technological. The changes we envision involve changing classrooms into effective educational environments for many more of the children who attend them. If the computer is to have any significant impact on education, it will be as part of broader pedagogical changes that make classrooms more engaging and exciting environments able to respond to a broader variety of learning differences in the students who inhabit them.

And how is this to happen? The key word for us is: "integration." This book is intended to make it easier and more valuable for you to integrate computers into the daily instruction that takes place in your classroom. The classroom is at the center of the school, the classroom teacher is at the center of the classroom, and this book is for you, the classroom teacher.

All authors have a particular audience in mind for their books. For us, the "you" for whom this book is intended is the "beginning" teacher. But we believe that there are two kinds of beginners in this field. On the one hand, we intend this book for beginners who have never been classroom teachers before. If you are taking a course as part of your preparation for becoming a teacher, you fit into this category. On the other hand, we intend this book to be very useful to experienced teachers who are novice computer-using teachers. If you are currently teaching, and are reading this book because you have a computer in your room that you know you aren't getting the most out of, you fit into this category.

So, if you are either of these kinds of beginners, you have come to the right book. We talk in plain language, not in bits and bytes. We talk more pedagogy than we talk technology. And we include a myriad of practical, easy-to-implement activities that you can immediately apply in your classroom, many of which do not even assume a specific piece of software.

Integrating Computers in Your Classroom is part of an eight-book series. In future years, we hope the success of these initial titles will enable us to add even more titles. Each book is designed to help teachers at specific grade levels integrate computers in their on-going classroom practice. Although you are reading just one of these books, we want you know that the series includes:

> *Integrating Computers in Your Classroom: Early Childhood,*
> *Integrating Computers in Your Classroom: Elementary Language Arts,*
> *Integrating Computers in Your Classroom: Elementary Math,*
> *Integrating Computers in Your Classroom: Elementary Science,*
> *Integrating Computers in Your Classroom: Elementary Grades,*
> *Integrating Computers in Your Classroom: Middle & Secondary English,*
> *Integrating Computers in Your Classroom: Middle & Secondary Math, and*
> *Integrating Computers in Your Classroom: Middle & Secondary Science*

The series nature of *Integrating Computers in Your Classroom* means a number of things. First, it means that all of the books in the series share certain commonalities. All the books share a common structure, comprised of essays, case studies, classroom activities, and bundled software.

Second, the series nature enables us to focus each book on an appropriately narrow area. This is especially true for the practical classroom activities which comprise Part II of each book. The result is that you will find a substantial number of practical activities which you can use in your classroom.

Part I: Essays and Case Studies

Each book in this series includes eighteen short essays, grouped into five chapters. Each essay is short, to the point, and simply stated. Each essay raises a single issue. All of them are intended to raise general issues, not issues specific to a particular content area or grade level. That is why, in fact, these essays appear in each of the books in the series.

The open-ended and occasionally irreverent questions that start off each essay may not all seem at first (or even second) glance to be immediately relevant to the specific material at hand. We include them because we want to encourage you to take a questioning attitude to what you are reading, as well as to what is currently going on with computers and schools. We believe that books for teachers, like software for students, are sometimes better when they occasionally raise questions without answering every single one of them, while providing you with additional resources with which to grapple with the questions.

Part I is the closest we get to theory. The essays lay out a framework for thinking about the integration of computers into ordinary classrooms. They reflect a set of values, both pedagogical and social/political. We hope they will provide a context that will help you utilize the more practical activities throughout the back half of the book more thoughtfully.

Part I is also practical. Therefore, we have concluded each chapter with a case study. The case studies illustrate practical implementation of at least one of the essays in that chapter. Unlike the essays–which raise general issues and are the same throughout all the books in the series–the case studies are examples of practical implementation. They are different for each book in the series and have been selected to illustrate specific examples of computer integration appropriate to the age-range and subject matter of each book.

Part II: Practical Classroom Activities

The back half of this book is comprised exclusively of practical classroom activities. In one sense, they are similar to the case studies, in that they illustrate examples of practical implementation. They are fundamentally different, however, from the case studies. A case study works well if it gives you a concrete sense of some successful strategies that classroom teachers can use to incorporate computer technology in their everyday classroom life. An activity works well if you can immediately put it to use.

We are also convinced that one of the major faults with the presentation of classroom activities in most education texts is the one-dimensional nature of that presentation. As a result, we utilize five different and distinct formats in presenting the activities at the back of these books:

Lesson Plan

This is the format most familiar to most teachers. It includes a series of categories (teacher preparation, materials needed, procedures, follow-up, and so forth) which structure the information. The Lesson Plan is the category which includes step-by-step instructions or procedures. We utilize this format when it is critical to know these detailed procedures.

Unit Plan

The Lesson Plan format is designed to describe a lesson that takes place over one or two days. The Unit Plan format is designed to describe a series of activities that take place over time, often a week or more. Each Unit Plan divides its materials into a small number of categories, categories which vary from unit plan to unit plan.

Up Front

We utilize two narrative formats to describe activities. The first of these is a first person account. In this "Up Front" format, the teacher doing the activity describes that activity. All the information you need to implement the activity is still included, but in a different, more personal style, with a focus on the reasons why a teacher has done certain things. Each Up Front account concludes with a set of Teacher Tips, designed to fill in some gaps left out of the narrative.

From the Sidelines

This is the second of the two narrative forms we use for describing activities: the third person account. In From the Sidelines, an observer in the classroom describes what is happening. We also have an observer with a real perspective: another teacher, a principal, a student, a newspaper reporter, a school board member, an interested parent, and so forth. Each account concludes with a Teacher's Response, where the teacher doing the activity can respond to what the observer has written. Some Teacher Responses are humorous, some argumentative, and often the teacher explains his or her reasons for doing what he or she did.

Kids' Perspective

The Kids' Perspective format allows students doing the activity to describe what happened, sometimes in their own words, sometimes through their work. Kids' Perspectives usually include samples of students' work to help you understand what is involved.

The classroom activities are not clustered separately into these five categories. We have purposely mixed up the activities to create some variety in what you are reading and to make it more enjoyable for you to "shop" through the various kinds of activities available.

Bundled Software

Integrating Computers in Your Classroom is dedicated to helping you integrate the use of computers in your own classroom, as well as other aspects of your professional life. As a result, we have bundled with this book a piece of *Lesson Planner* software.

The *Lesson Planner* software functions in two important ways. First, it functions as a tutorial. There is a series of on-screen tutorials–called Guides–designed to walk you through the process of preparing a lesson plan. The Guides help you look at the sources for lesson plans, the importance of a planning and brainstorming stage, the need to get ideas on screen and into a file, the ways in which those initial ideas can be organized and structured, and so forth. The software also includes Practice Files which provide a number of lesson plan templates. All of these pedagogical components are included with an easy-to-use word processor, which you use to write your lesson plans.

At some point, of course, you will no longer need the tutorial and the program turns into a tool which you can use to write your lesson plans. The software includes an on-line database of twenty activities. You can search through this database (for all the spreadsheet activities) or simply browse through the activities. When you find one around which you want to build a lesson plan, you can electronically copy it into your word processing file.

At the same time, the *Lesson Planner* software allows you to add your own activities. You can use the software as a way to store your best activity ideas, because the database nature of the program allows for both easy storage and easy retrieval. And you will have the power of the software to build lesson plans around your own favorite activities while becoming more comfortable with using computers and more aware of their power and utility within your classroom.

About This Book

Many secondary school math teachers did not enter the field with an extensive academic background in mathematics. So it's not surprising that the computer is being used increasingly in secondary classrooms to help meet new and more demanding national standards for the teaching of mathematics. But is it being used more imaginatively? Is it being *integrated* in a way that exploits its power to help the classroom teacher move the quality of instruction to a new plateau? Is it helping to get students excited about figuring things out on their own? Are teachers taking advantage of the evident ability of computer use to strengthen their own sense of mathematics?

We have tried to address these issues in this book. We believe that the biggest challenge to computer-using classroom teachers is how to fit computers as seamlessly as possible into an "enlightened" math curriculum—one that encourages students to become explorers and manipulators of information and ideas, improves attitudes toward learning math, and makes learning math more exciting. Computer use often also seems to have the ability to stimulate more collaborative relationships with fellow teachers.

The activities in Part II have been selected not just for their ability to provide concrete, ideas of how to integrate computers in your math curriculum on Monday morning, but also to illustrate "higher-order" uses of computers in the math classroom: giving students real life problems to solve, ensuring that they're able to use math in their daily lives, giving them insights into the methods that real mathematicians use in their quest for answers.

We hope this book serves the needs of teachers looking for an approach to learning that allows students to learn and apply the traditional, basic "mathematics knowledge," play an active role in the learning process, and get more exposure to higher order skills and problem-solving. We also hope that teachers relatively new to computer integration, after using this book, will find it easier to think of ways to use computers for a variety of other purposes, including:

- providing concrete and immediate visual representations to math concepts, as a way of improving students' conceptual understanding;
- using computer technology as an instrument for implementing new and "higher order" goals embedded in the standards of the NCTM;
- using interactive software to support an inquiry model of learning where students function as co-manipulators, rather than inactive recipients, of concepts and information;
- integrating computers, inquiry methods of learning, and cooperative learning to create a new classroom dynamic that puts more responsibility in the hands of students;
- providing students with experiences that are project-based; and
- using multiple math teaching strategies in response to multiple student learning styles.

PART I

"This book focuses on the practical ways that computers can create a significant, positive impact on thousands of classrooms.

   ◆ It is not about using computers to replace teachers.
   ◆ It is not about using computers in laboratory situations."

First Principles

Dear Dr. DeLeet:

I have been teaching for twelve years and I am just now getting around to using computers in my classroom (the high school bought new Macs, and sent down these old Apple IIs to our middle school). My problem is that now my principal seems to expect me to perform miracles with these machines. I don't get it. It was hard enough to find the time to meet all the other new "mandates" that have been forced down our throats in the last few years. How am I supposed to know how to use these things? Where will I get the time to learn? Why is this so important, anyway?

A Fed-up Veteran

CHAPTER 1

Computers Within Classrooms

- What if they gave a revolution and no one came?
- What kind of revolution is this, anyway?
- Is this steak, or just sizzle?

The faculty of a rural high school in Tennessee is gathered together for an afternoon in-service session on "Making More Effective Use of Our Computer Resources." The trainer hands the teachers sheets of paper asking them to choose their "top two" ways to complete the following sentence:

MORE CLASSROOM TEACHERS WILL USE COMPUTERS WHEN:

(a) they learn how to use them to develop higher order thinking skills;

(b) they learn how to use them to promote learning by doing;

(c) they learn how to use them to respond to student differences in learning styles;

(d) they learn how to use them to encourage cooperative learning;

(e) they learn how to use them to give students a chance to practice, practice, practice things like fraction conversion, multiplication, and area measurement;

(f) they learn how to use them to help students improve their scores on standardized basic skill exams;

(g) they learn how to use them to promote learning by teaching.

[See the end of this essay for their top two choices. What do you think they were?]

America's schools have been caught up in the "computer revolution" for at least fifteen years. So, why is there a growing sense that this revolution has fizzled? Why do so many experts say that the impact of 18-20 billion dollars worth of technology investments on the basic operation of most classrooms is "practically nil?" What kind of revolution is this, anyway?

The Failed Revolution

One clue to this mystery involves the simple question: Where? We know that most school learning still takes place inside ordinary, "self-contained" classrooms. So whether most children develop adequate skills depends on what happens *within* these classrooms. There is also evidence that computers can provide valuable classroom support in teaching subjects that are at the core of the curriculum. Yet study after study shows that schools use computers primarily as drill and practice machines, or as "toys" offering rewards for good behavior. And far too often, even these uninspiring interventions occur outside the boundaries of the regular classroom, in laboratories, media centers, and other ill-named "sanctuaries."

History may offer another clue to the lost revolution. Computers began showing up in schools in the 1950's and 1960's, accompanied by rumblings of impending revolution. These new marvels first appeared in school offices and computer labs. They were networked, utilized time-sharing on mainframes over modems, and were run by the computer expert. They fizzled. In the late 1970's and early 1980's, "personal" computers entered the schools with even greater fanfare. These were simpler machines which individual teachers and their students could use within their own classrooms, buying individual pieces of software to support the core activity of the classroom. By the late 1980's, however, personal computers had rediscovered their mainframe roots; and more and more drifted away to computer labs and central offices. Once again they were networked, distanced from teachers, and run by network specialists.

What This Book is NOT

This book focuses on the practical ways that computers can create a significant, positive impact on thousands of classrooms.

- ◆ It is not about marginalizing the use of computers in schools, nor about using computers for administrative purposes, by either administrators or teachers.
- ◆ It is not about using computers as the electronic equivalent of the Friday afternoon movie, to keep kids quiet for a couple of hours.
- ◆ It is not about using computers as drill-and-practice machines.
- ◆ It is not about using computers to replace teachers.
- ◆ It is not about teaching computer literacy.
- ◆ It is not about using the computer to support hardware manufacturers' search for new markets.
- ◆ It is not about using computers as a reward. It is not about letting students play games after successfully completing "real" work.
- ◆ It is not about using computers in laboratory situations.

What This Book IS

This book is about using computers inside real classrooms. This book is funda-

mentally a practical book. If you are training to be a teacher, it will help you
see the computer as an invaluable tool in your future profession. If you are
already a teacher, it will help you get beyond the fear of the computer as an
esoteric device useful only to those who know its innards. This is a book to read
and enjoy, but it is even more a book for you to put to practical use.

◆   It is about integrating computers in your classroom. It is about help-
     ing you use whatever computer resources are available to you.

◆   It is about helping you see the connection between educational soft-
     ware and the other curriculum materials you utilize.
◆   It is about tying computer use to major curriculum goals. It is about
     supporting your core efforts within your classroom with effective and
     innovative educational software.
◆   It is about using the computer as a tool to promote student learning
     within the regular curriculum. It is about using the computer as a
     tool to help your students learn about anything and everything. It is
     about using software "productivity tools" to learn about all school
     subjects.

◆ It is about using computers in cooperative and innovative ways and supporting the varied learning styles of all your students.
◆ It is about new ways to use computers to help your weaker students gain basic skills.

The essays which make up most of Part I provide an intellectual context within which to practice sensible computer integration. Interspersed among these essays are specific case studies that exemplify actual ways in which people are practicing what this book preaches. Part II is probably the most practical part of this book. It is full of classroom activities, described from various points of view (teachers, parents, students, principals, etc.) And the software "bundled" with the book has been designed as a convenient tool to help you write lesson plans and save lesson ideas for future reference.

[The teachers in Tennessee chose (c) how to respond to learning styles differences and (f) how to help students improve their scores on standardized basic skill exams, as their top two goals.

What We Emphasize and Why

• **Should kids be required to wear white coats in computer labs?**
• **Are productivity tools capitalist tools?**
• **Are some computers more equal than others?**

A computer coordinator in a large Santa Monica middle school is describing her frustration at the way classroom teachers in her system use computers when they finally get around to "allowing" them within the hallowed walls of their classrooms. "Most teachers," she reports, "think of computers as extras, not tools of their trade. The kind of thing I hear them say to their students most often is: 'If you finish your WORK, I'll let you go to the computer corner and PLAY with AlgeBlaster.'"

What computers can do is impressive; what schools use computers for is often trivial. Even schools that try to use computers to achieve key instructional goals still usually try to do it by pulling students out of regular classrooms into a segregated environment. The computer becomes a subject rather than a tool, and most teachers are allowed to avoid confronting the need to learn how to put this new "tool of their trade" to practical use. This basic situation has shaped the priorities and emphases of this book.

Computers Within Classrooms

The classroom teacher is still the one who delivers the core learning that takes place in schools. To locate computers outside of the classroom–the central context of the school–trivializes computers and their potential for change. Computer labs are easy and (supposedly) cost-effective ways to put computers in schools, which may be why administrators and hardware manufacturers gravitate towards them. Computer labs are not *inherently* irrelevant, but they minimize, encapsulate, thus impeding the computer from playing a more central role in the educational process you, as the classroom teacher, are responsible for mediating. Computer labs also maintain the "mystery" of the common ordinary computer–which needs to be demystified in most schools–and can keep instructional and pedagogical decisions in the hands of people whose primary skills are technological rather than educational. For all these reasons, this book emphasizes integrating computers in your classroom.

Classrooms With 1-3 Computers

There is no good reason to ponder the ideal number of computers in a single classroom. The number of computers in your classroom will probably not, in the near future (if ever), be dictated by reason; the number will be dictated by budgetary realities. Those realities indicate that you can expect to have between one and three computers...at most. Since this book is designed to help you deal with the most likely practical realities you will confront within your classroom, most of the "What Do I Do Monday Morning" activities at the back of this book assume that you will have a limited number of computers in your classroom.

Cooperative Learning

One of the most common misconceptions about computers is that they are ideal instruments for *individual* learning. Clearly, that use of computers may sometimes be legitimate in theory, and is common in practice. But you know that solo learning is often not the most appropriate or effective pedagogical strategy. Too often computers are used to "atomize" and isolate students from each other. Cooperative learning has become a central pedagogy in many classrooms, for its instructional, social, and motivational benefits. The computer may well prove far more effective in cooperative learning settings than in individualized learning situations. The cooperative approach both humanizes the computer and integrates its use into common and important educational practice. That is why we place such an emphasis on using the computer in the context of cooperative learning experiences.

Accommodating Diversity

Why does this book emphasize the computer as an asset to meeting the needs of diverse students? A clear problem in contemporary American education is that it too rarely acknowledges, fosters, and takes advantage of the diversity with which it is increasingly confronted. Some educators even blame diversity for their own failures, instead of looking to diversity as a springboard for increasing their success.

Computers can provide you with a rich variety of teaching strategies, accommodating to widely divergent learning styles, multiple intelligences, and special learning needs within your classroom. The atmosphere in today's classroom often reinforces the tendency to teach to the linguistic, logical-mathematical, and intrapersonal learner and virtually ignore the other "intelligences" that students possess. This tendency misses the chance to validate and develop all the intelligences of all children and fails to take advantage of the likelihood that the more ways a subject is presented, the better that subject is learned. The reason for extending computer activities to reach all the intelligences is very simple: you can better utilize the match between the resources you have, the way you use them, and the dominant intelligences of your students.

In the hands of a gifted teacher, computers are thus not just tools to accommodate or adapt to ONE other kind of student learner, but to a number of different kinds of learners. With the right software, the computer can become a tool for responding to the needs of students who do better when they can visualize the concrete manifestations of a mathematics operation (as with Ventura's *Hands-On Math* series), or a student who needs more practice in the way to set up the solution to math word problems (*Outnumbered*), or a student with a physical or learning disability who needs shortcuts in keyboarding (Hartley's *My Words*, Don Johnston's *Predict It*), etc. Computers can provide your students who have learning disabilities or physical handicaps entry points to learning and communicating they have never before experienced in schools.

With respect to students with special needs, it is important to note that the student who is fully integrated in the regular classroom can thrive in a number of important ways (academic, social, psychological, etc.) as a result of that integration, and that computers can be effective tools for facilitating the kind of integration that prevents students with special needs from becoming "islands in the mainstream." Such students can be given special roles, for example, in cooperative learning activities around the computer. Giving students with special needs roles as cross-age computer tutors of younger students enables them to gain in self-esteem, and raise their own academic achievement while relearning some skills they may not have completely mastered first time around. Most important, from the point of view of the classroom teacher, the classroom computer can make it easier to deal successfully with the learning differences of students with special needs.

Productivity Tools

Why does this book include so many classroom activities that use spreadsheets, word processors and other productivity tools? In a word–access. Even if your school has a very limited software budget, you can usually obtain productivity tools. Productivity tools can be used effectively for learning activities across the entire curriculum. They can be used easily by students from the elementary grades through high school. And, since such tools are used in real life in a variety of home and job-related contexts, using them in your school for instructional purposes has the added benefit of helping your students learn to use tools they will need in their adult lives.

Thinking Skills

Why does this book place such an emphasis on thinking skills? As our society changes more rapidly and becomes ever more complex, mastering a static body of knowledge becomes less critical than the ability to analyze and process new information about key content areas. Throughout the curriculum, from science and math to language arts and social studies, teachers are beginning to focus on the skills their students need to understand and work with that content. In addition, once students master certain higher order thinking skills, they seem to achieve at higher levels in future grades. The computer may not be a great tool for *acquiring* information, but it is a fantastic resource for utilizing and manipulating information. That is why we place such an emphasis on thinking skills.

What Research Says to the Teacher

- **You can lead a school to software, but you cannot make it compute.**
- **Will the mice play when the sage gets off the stage?**
- **Does software have to be used as a dessert?**

The superintendent has gathered together his "leadership team" to begin discussing the next "five-year plan" for the use of technology in a large California school system. The expert he has brought in starts by displaying a series of quotes taken from the recent research literature on computers and schools. Some of the statements had been altered to reverse their meaning; some were direct quotations from the literature. The teachers were asked to guess which were the "original statements" and which were "fraudulent reversals" of the original. Can you sort out the true findings?

1. *The effects of Computer Based Instruction seem especially clear in studies promoting the development of basic academic skills with pupils who have traditionally been classified as "disadvantaged."*

2. *The most consequential finding in the body of literature regarding IBM's Writing to Read is that its use in the development of writing skills is significantly different from an individual teacher's use of the process approach to writing within a traditional classroom environment.*

3. *A 1990 University of Michigan study reported that children can gain the equivalent of three months of instruction per school year when computers are available to them.*

4. *Students in both the cooperative and the competitive conditions performed lower on an achievement test than did the students in the individualistic [i.e. one-on-one] condition.*

5. *The LOGO computer programming language has been described as an environment in which children will develop problem-solving skills. Unfortunately, much of the research concerned with LOGO and problem-solving has not found such connection.*

The team had trouble sorting out which statements were fraudulent reversals (numbers 2 and 4 above).

Does knowing about the research makes any difference, for policymakers or teachers? Importantly, it does, because the research is pointing in a very clear direction. Unfortunately, it is the road NOT taken by most school systems. What some of the research says to you as a teacher is that you could be using software to get a lot more help achieving important classroom objectives than you may realize from the way computers are presently being used in your school.

How Can Computers Help?

Before most teachers, or principals, are likely to take the time, energy, and effort required to learn about effective uses of computers within classrooms, they need to know whether it is worth it. As Larry Cuban has cogently demonstrated, most teachers will utilize new technologies only to the degree that they believe that these technologies will help them solve problems that *they* define as important. Cuban also suggests that schools usually go through a consistent cyclical pattern in their response to new technologies: (1) exhilaration, (2) scientific credibility, (3) disappointment, and (4) blame. (*Harvard Ed. Review*, 2/89.)

Currently available research and evaluation studies does yet draw definitive conclusions about the ultimate potential of computers as a tool used wisely within the regular classroom. But they do provide tantalizing evidence that in certain areas, the computer has already demonstrated its capacity to provide invaluable support in helping teachers accomplish goals that they themselves define as crucial to their success.

Are Computers Being Used Well?

What does the research say? Presently schools use computers primarily as individualized drill and practice machines, or (occasionally) as extracurricular enrichment tools, not as tools to support basic learning. Students from poorer communities and underachieving students often get less access to computers.

And when they *do* get access, they are too often confined to drill and practice and tutorial activities. (H.J. Becker, *Communications of the ACM*, 1983.)

Another lost opportunity comes because of teachers and administrators who consider computers one-on-one learning devices; the advantages of having students work together around a computer are neglected. Students who do get to work in small groups are rarely taught specific skills and roles for cooperative learning, with the result that many of the major benefits of small group work around the computer are still lost.

Researchers who look at the use of computers in schools are coming to the following conclusions:

1. Although schools have bought lots of computers, most of these machines cannot impact classroom instruction, because they do not end up inside classrooms.
2. When computers do make it into the classroom, they are rarely used in ways that tie in closely with basic instruction, so that they can not be expected to significantly impact that instruction.

3. Wherever the computers are, their use is marginal to the core of instruction going on in classrooms.
4. Even when an effort is made to connect computer work to the core curriculum, the connections are often superficial or peripheral.
5. When computers are integrated into the basic life of the classroom in meaningful ways, they seem to have the power to make a significant difference in the effectiveness of classroom instruction.

Research and Styles of Teaching

A second indicator of the potential of classroom computers involves their use as a part of a broader series of changes designed to help teachers move away from "lectern" styles of teaching to other forms of classroom organization that involve small group learning, peer tutoring, learning stations, cooperative learning, and the like.

Computer-based activities, such as simulations and many tool uses, make small-group problem-solving by students possible. Teachers can manage groups of students, rather than conduct the more typical whole-class activity. As Jan Hawkins and Karen Sheingold point out, managing and supporting such work effectively requires observational skills different from those teachers normally apply, and new intuitions about when and how to intervene in student-based activities, as well as how to monitor the progress of individual students. ("Computers and the Organization of Learning," in Culbertson, *et.al.*, *Microcomputers in Education*, 1986.)

Research and Achievement

A third set of studies relates directly to the use of computers in heterogeneous classrooms in helping underachievers to raise their basic skill levels:

◆ Children on the lower end of achievement scales seem to benefit the most from using computers. (Lillie, *et.al.*, *Computers and Effective Instruction*, 1989.)
◆ Computers can reduce student learning time in many subject areas.
◆ The use of word processing by children as young as third- and fourth-graders can produce striking changes in their attitudes towards writing. (Riel, *Journal of Educational Computing Research*, 1985, p. 317-377.)
◆ Students can learn math skills more quickly and cost effectively when instruction is supplemented by the use of computers than with tradi-

tional instruction. (Center for Advanced Technology in Education, University of Oregon.)

Research and Diversity

One clue to the potential of computers involves their use as a tool for helping teachers accommodate greater diversity in learning abilities and styles within a single classroom. Lynne Outhred points out that use of the word processor results in children writing longer and better stories, with greater willingness to revise their work. In a study in the *Journal of Learning Disabilities* (April, 1989), she reports that children with learning disabilities had fewer spelling errors and increased the length of their written efforts. Holz, using computers to teach basic money-handling skills to trainable mentally handicapped students (ages 7-20), found achievement differences to be statistically significant in favor of those using computers.

Research and Learning

Computers seem able to improve problem-solving skills in a wide variety of situations: e.g., at preschool levels, in conjunction with cooperative learning, for third and fifth graders trying to improve their math concept skills, in conjunction with the use of simulation software. Computers have also been shown to enhance students' motivation to learn and their attitude towards the subject matter, as well as student interaction and the amount of "on-task verbal activity" that occurs among students. Finally, research indicates that the relationship between teacher and student is central to successful computer-mediated education, and that the most "successful" teachers are "orchestrators," who integrate and coordinate computer activities with other means of instruction.

Case Study ▬

Three Not So Easy Pieces

Alexander Woodward is a high school teacher who turned to computers as a tool to revitalize his classroom. His efforts to improve led him
through alternative software choices, to inquiry methods, and finally to
a classroom structure that merged all the pieces with cooperative
learning. He discovered that:
- learner-centered, interactive software can support an inquiry
  model of learning where students function as co-manipulators
  rather than inactive recipients of information,
- integrating computers, inquiry methods of learning, and cooperative learning can create a new classroom dynamic that
  puts more responsibility into the hands of students,
- a cooperative learning structure can help promote the role of
  the teacher as a "guide on the side" facilitator, instead of a
  "sage on the stage" director.

As his classes got smaller over the years, Alexander
Woodward began to notice the students more. In terms of curriculum mastery, he began to see that it wasn't just a matter of getting
it or not. There were gray areas. He started talking to students
about their mistakes and learned that often "good thinking" went
into wrong answers. He wasn't quite sure what he could do to
improve the situation, but he started with the computer and the
Supposer Series.

Initially, he stood in front of his classes and used the software
for demonstration. It worked. Kids were less bored and he was
more interesting. He might have stopped there if it hadn't been for a
couple of "eager beaver" students. They began coming to use the
software after school. They convinced him that they could use it to
create their own intuitive solutions to math problems.

He had never considered that students could be successful
without his careful leadership. However, here before his eyes were
some students doing just that. For days, he ruminated on this
discovery. It appeared that this software fostered, almost automatically, an inquiry approach to math. The students were

constructing and manipulating objects and shapes. When they changed a factor or premise (i.e., when they "supposed"something new) they could immediately see the impact on the computer screen. The kids were really turned on. Inadvertently, he had stumbled on something, but what was it?

To figure it out, he decided to create an inquiry approach for all his students. He arranged for the students to go to the computer lab and use the *Supposer* software. It seemed like a great idea, but it resulted mostly in organized chaos. Only some did well. Others were lost and confused. Some kids seemed almost hostile that he wasn't running the show. This wasn't working the way he had pictured it. Something was still missing, but what was it?

That's when he plunged into cooperative learning. Instead of placing individuals at a computer, he began to make the computer part of a larger group activity. He stopped sending kids to the computer lab and got busy rearranging his classroom. He started with two computers and divided the class into several small groups. The results of this strategy were better, but still not good enough for him. So he looked for different software. Along with the *Supposer* series, he found TERC (Technology Education Research Center) software like *Connectany*.

Ultimately, Mr. Woodward discovered that improvements in student work seemed to depend most directly on how well he managed the group structure. He began to pay more serious attention to how he grouped the kids. At first, they had just got together in groups of friends. Now, he created the groups to include a diversity of student attributes.

He recognized that kids need more than just being placed together. They need techniques for working together. He assigned them specific well-defined roles in their groups. He moved among groups and gently encouraged them to jump the problem hurdles. He added debriefing sessions after each lesson.

Finally, all three pieces seemed to fit together: the computer (with appropriate software), the new inquiry approach, and the students (working cooperatively). Computer technology has made mathematics a "hands on" dynamic operation for students in his classes. Now his students "do" math, instead of sitting and listening while math concepts are explained.   ▄▄▄▄▄■

"COMPUTERS CAN BE VERY POWERFUL TOOOOLS!"

"Hardware and software each provide their problems for teachers, but the two components are different, with different solutions to their problems."

The Resources at Hand

Dear Dr. DeLeet:

I am in my last year of graduate school here at the Michigan State Department Of Sociology (MS-DOS), with a minor in Education and just received word that my application to teach sixth grade next year here in inner-city Glancing has been accepted. My problem is that they have told me that my sixth grade class will have access to only two Apple IIE's that sit outside in the corridor, and I've used only IBM's to write my papers and stuff here at MS-DOS. (I did get an A- in my computer literacy course, but I still don't think I know much about using these things with kids.) My question is: Will it be worth my while to spend the time to learn how to use these old machines in my hectic first year of teaching?

A Fearful Rookie

Getting Started

- **Begin what is difficult where it is easy?**
- **Where have all the old tools gone?**
- **Is computer illiteracy a badge of honor?**

Anita Stewert could not believe what was happening to her. She had been teaching for 28 years, and she considered herself an excellent teacher. And now her principal was asking her–demanding, it seemed–to integrate computers into her ninth-grade math classroom. She did not know a thing about them; in fact, she had never used a computer herself in her life. Never felt the need, and did not feel it now.

"I don't even know if I approve of computers," she told the principal. "I'm afraid they will make my classroom too impersonal. From everything I hear, they're difficult to use, foreboding, and unforgiving. Do not even bother pretending that they are teacher-friendly, hassle-free aids. As far as I can tell, computers have earned their bad reputation."

Starting to use computers inside a classroom where they have not been used before is not an easy task. Consciously, semi-consciously, sometimes even subconsciously, you may be mulling over some of these questions: Do I really have time for this? Is it worth the effort? How am I going to manage the logistics? Will it upset my existing classroom dynamics in some unexpected way? Is it possible to truly *integrate* these machines? Where to begin?

In addition, you may not know your way around computers; you may not know whether you really like them or approve of them; and you may not even feel comfortable expressing your ambivalence, or even admitting it to yourself. And computers have sometimes earned a bad reputation. They *can* sometimes be difficult to use, and unforgiving, while all the while someone in authority is pretending they are these teacher-friendly, hassle-free "aids." What is needed are some easier ways of integrating computers into classrooms, and some straight talk about the very real barriers that still exist.

This book is for teachers who are ready to take advantage of a newly available tool to make classroom teaching better–and more fun–but who need some practical ways to get started. Getting started is not as easy as some administrators pretend, but it is not nearly as difficult as many teachers think. In the essays, case studies, practical classroom activities, and bundled software of this book, you'll find what you need to get started.

It may be difficult for you to separate the wheat from the chaff among the available software products, especially when so much of it is so bad, and so much of what is popular is pedagogically shallow. From the outset, some persistent, if unspoken, computer stereotypes need to be set straight.

◆ Computers are not drill and practice machines.

◆ They do not serve much purpose if they are used just for "enrichment" or fluff.

◆ They do not represent a new subject to teach, but rather a new tool to *teach existing subjects.*

Software

Hardware and software each provide their problems for teachers, but the two components are different,with different solutions to their problems.

Part II of this book describes a wide variety of classroom activities that use software with certain desired characteristics, including:

(1) that it fits easily and directly into curriculum priorities for most teachers to teach, rather than representing some new and different subject matter,

(2) that it lends itself easily to use in small groups, as well as occasional "whole class" lessons,

(3) that it motivates students, encourages active learning, and promotes higher-order thinking skills,

(4) that it is easy to get started on, for both children and teachers,

(5) that it is flexible and versatile, so that it can be used in different ways,

(6) that it is readily available to teachers around the country,

(7) that it does not require lots of expensive equipment to use, and

(8) that the same software, or a reasonable "facsimile," is available for the computers commonly available in schools.

One key criterion for selecting each classroom computer integration activity in Part II of this book is how easy the software in it will be for you to use. Look for software that is easy to get started on. For example, if you have never used a word processor, do not start with *WordPerfect*; start with *Bank Street Writer*, a word processor designed for teachers and students. When you want an integrated product–something that combines a word processor, spreadsheet, and database programs–do not start with *Microsoft Works*, a product designed for business. Start with *MindPlay Works*, a product designed explicitly for schools.

Another good idea is to find a piece of software that one of your students is already familiar with, such as *Where in the World is Carmen Sandiego?*. Starting with *Carmen*, you can have the students who have already learned how to use it teach other students, or you. This strategy helps you learn how to use more software and helps your students feel good about what they already know.

Hardware

It is difficult to talk about hardware because your school has what it has, and you must make do with whatever is available. But if there is a choice, many teachers have found that it is easier to begin on a Macintosh than on other computers. Each piece of hardware has some advantages over the other, and this book includes many ideas for using Apple II's or MS-DOS machines, but it is generally accepted that the Macintosh is the easiest for most people to get used to quickly, and with the least emotional stress (for example, feeling stupid).

A useful strategy is to ask your school if you can to borrow a computer to take home. For years, people have been encouraging schools to let teachers take computers home on weekends and vacations, in order to become familiar with the machines. You can take the classroom software along with the computer and become comfortable with it before you have to use it with your students.

The One-Computer Classroom

- **When is one enough?**
- **It take one to "no" one.**
- **What is one to do?**

Jim Smith, a new ninth grade teacher in a small suburban school, was dismayed to discover that he had only one computer for his entire class, and an old Apple IIe at that. Last year, he had "student-taught" in a school where every classroom had four computers, two of which were brand-new Macintoshes. "What good will one computer do me?" he thought. "I learned how to integrate three or four of them in lots of classroom activities, but what can I do with just one?"

Jim's situation represents one kind of one-computer classroom problem, because he enters the teaching profession feeling confident that he knows how to integrate three or four computers in a classroom. He must use his experience in the multi-computer classroom to figure out how to integrate one computer into his teaching. What is he to do, with just one? You, on the other hand, may be faced with the other one-computer classroom problem: going from none to one. Both of these problems are important because it is most realistic that you will only have one computer in your classroom for the foreseeable future.

How can this be? Presently there are an average of two computers for every 25-30 students in our schools. Since the average class size in America is somewhere in the mid 20's, you might think that most teachers would not have to deal with a situation where they have only one computer for an entire class. Many classroom teachers are lucky to have even one computer available for classroom use, and often that one computer has to be shared with others.

Reasons for this situation vary. Computers are unevenly distributed: between secondary and elementary schools, between affluent areas and poor areas, and so forth. Additionally, within many schools, computers are often locked in media centers, computer laboratories, computer rooms, and the like, so the number available for truly integrated use within the regular classroom shrinks even further.

Therefore, for a long time you will need to know how to take the most advantage of the single computer in your classroom. Luckily, many individual teachers have demonstrated that even a single computer, in the hands of a typical, but competent, teacher can be put to significant advantage in advancing common classroom learning goals.

Knowing how to use one computer to serve an entire classroom simultaneously (rather than a few children at a time) is important to the whole idea of computer integration. A book like *Great Teaching in the One Computer Classroom* (Tom Snyder Productions) can help teachers get a lot more mileage out of a single computer, by illustrating the way the projected computer can be used to introduce new topics, stimulate discussion and debate, or launch a lesson that then continues off the computer.

Some Practical Suggestions

What follows are a number of suggestions for taking advantage of a single computer in your classroom.

1. You can use a computer as a more active and versatile blackboard. Using inexpensive and readily-available connecting devices, you can attach an Apple II computer to a classroom TV monitor, and display the computer screen to your entire class at once. You can then make the blackboard come alive with graphic illustrations, have your students do "board work" that the other students in your class can observe, or run software that readily lends itself to "whole-class" activities. The idea of being able to use the computer to help introduce a new topic to the whole class, of sending children "up" to the projected computer as a substitute blackboard in math, or of using the computer as a dynamic presentation tool, is important, because it helps you recognize how versatile a teaching tool even one computer can be, giving you more incentive to learn how to use it. To connect an Apple II to a classroom TV monitor requires an RGB connector available at Radio Shack, and a few connecting wires. Total cost: about $40.00. (A similar device for the Macintosh is available in the $300 range.)

2. You can use a single computer as a back-of-the-room work station to which you can send two, three, or four students while the rest of your class is working on something else. You can set up a Macintosh in the back of the room (the Mac-in-Back), for example, so that some of your students can be doing independent writing tasks (e.g., adding to a story in process) or skill-related tasks (e.g., peer-tutoring on math word problems), while you are engaged in a whole-class lesson with the rest of the class.

3.   For a somewhat greater investment, you can project an enlarged computer screen. The "Macboard" provides certain advantages over projections of other computers: the size of type on the screen can be quickly and easily enlarged to ensure that everybody in the class can read it; the Macintosh can be set up to read the words on the screen aloud; sound effects can be added; etc.

4.   You can cycle groups of 4–6 students through a computer center in your classroom while the rest of your class does other small-group, cooperative activities. Or you can teach whole-class activities to the rest of your class, while a small group (perhaps including those children who can benefit most from a set of different activities on the computer) works independently at the computer.

5.   You can use software designed specifically for the one-computer classroom (e.g., software from Tom Snyder Productions).

6. You can use a single computer as a peer tutoring tool. Having teams of two students to introduce 2-4 other students to a particular piece of software, provides important benefits to all involved.

7. You can send your single computer home with parents for long weekends and vacations. One computer can, for example, be circulated among families of underachieving students in your class, with software–appropriate for family enjoyment–to help raise skill levels.

8. Your one-computer classroom can have a computer center as one of a number of learning centers which you create, through which your students regularly cycle. Others centers might include an art center, a writing center, and so forth.

Telecommunications: A Special Case

Telecommunications, where available, can also help you get the most out of a single computer in your classroom. With an inexpensive modem, access to a telephone line, and the appropriate (and not expensive) communications software, you and your students can communicate with one another, or with experts and researchers who are helping to give a particular exploration authenticity, across small or vast geographic boundaries. Writing by modem to students at a school in Colorado or South Carolina helps build skills in writing as a way to communicate. It accustoms them to writing in a context more meaningful for most than traditional school writing assignments from the teacher. Your students can collaborate on projects and reports with students from around the country.

Although the "relatively" inexpensive materials needed for telecommunications may be beyond your practical reach, some examples of the ways that it is already being used may illustrate its potential. The National Geographic Society's *Kids Network* project uses computing and telecommunications for elementary school children to collect and process scientific data (e.g., about acid rain) and transmit their findings across the country. Students become part of an exciting scientific investigation that helps develop skills in doing science, calculating results, writing about it, and appreciating its complexities. Students with learning disabilities in Hawaii are paired with "pen pals" in the Midwest in a situation that promotes meaningful writing experience and produces significant achievement gains. Using an on-line subscription service called the World Classroom, students in Rhode Island accessed and analyzed data from the National Earthquake Center, enabling them to predict the San Francisco earthquake of the late 1980's shortly before it occurred.

Telecommunications can help prepare your students to use real-life data to make real-life decisions about themselves, their environment, and their world. It will also eventually provide access for them to the proposed national information superhighway. Since full-motion video, as well as text, graphics, and sound, will soon move easily into classrooms over networks, the potential of telecommunications, especially in the one-computer classroom, is enormous.

The Multiple-Computer Classroom

- **The guide at the side or the sage on the stage?**
- **Why put off until tomorrow what you can get your students to do for you today?**
- **Is two *too* much?**

The three groups of eighth graders on the computers are using Solve It! American History Mysteries *to hunt down a spy in Boston in 1775, during the revolution. The three groups working off the computers are brainstorming letters they are going to write that pretend to be from an eleven-year-old son of Sam Adams, describing what life has been like in his house for the past few months. Halfway through the time period, the groups switch; and the groups who have been doing prewriting brainstorming off the computers begin drafting their letters on the computers. Meanwhile, the children who have been trying to hunt down the spy have to fill out a questionnaire that gets them to think about the problem-solving techniques and math skills they used in their quest for the spy. The next day, the groups reverse tasks on a similar assignment.*

If you have access to two or three computers, you can explore the many ways in which you can cycle groups of 2-5 students through a set of computer activities while other groups (or the rest of your class as a whole) are engaged in a set of related, off-computer activities. Of the many different models for this type of classroom organization, here are just a couple: (1) Two groups do computer activity A; two groups do related activity B; and two other groups do another, related activity C. (2) One group is off and one group on the three computers for the entire period; the next day they reversed roles; etc. etc. The multiple-computer situation helps you reap the benefits of taking the classroom spotlight off yourself as teacher and focus it on your students as active learners.

Most of the ideas useful in the one-computer classroom can be applied in the two-computer, or three-computer classroom. As computers are added, a greater degree of flexibility becomes available. Since most classrooms today or tomorrow will have just one, two, or three computers, you will need to learn more "off and on strategies," i.e., ways to orchestrate your class where some of your students work together at a computer while others do not.

The Two-Computer Classroom

Two computers can be used well when you set up learning centers in different areas of the classroom. You can make each a center or put them together in a subject-specific center (e.g., the "computer writing center"). Two computers could also be used to deal with the problem of teaching to the "norm," by teaming some higher–achieving children with some lower-achieving ones as peer tutors (with three or four students at each computer while you work with the rest of your class in a whole).

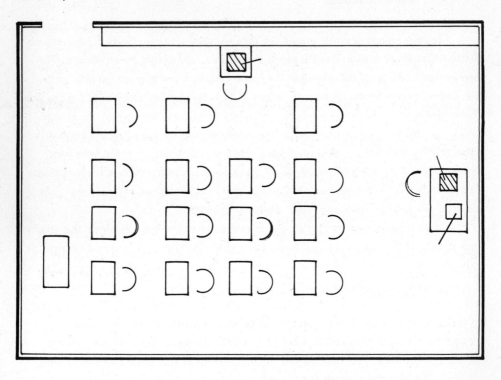

The more software is integrated with the subject matter of the curriculum, the more opportunities exist for cycling groups of students on and off the computer as a part of a lesson that includes some small group activities that require computer use and some that do not. Database activities are a good example, where some of your students can be getting the data they need to enter or analyze (through interviews, encyclopedias, etc.) while others are use the computers for data entry or analysis.

The Three-Computer Classroom

The three computer classroom is probably the minimum needed to make sure that ALL students get some time at the computer during a single classroom lesson or period. Let's say you have twenty-four students in your classroom. If half your class is working in groups of four at the three computers, the other twelve students can be working in three other groups of four on some related non-computer task. Then, halfway through the activity, the on-the-computer groups can switch with the off-the-computer groups.

Three computers can also be effectively utilized in three different learning centers. A first-grade teacher in Tennessee who had six different centers–reading, writing, art, numbers, the city, and science–put a computer in those for writing, art, and science.

Some educators complain that the computer will have no meaning until a computer sits in front of every student. Others counter that such a situation would be the worst thing imaginable. The argument is moot. For the next decade (or more) the reality is that you cannot expect to have more than three computers in your classroom (and you probably cannot hope for even as many as three). Three computers is (as the activities in Part II of this book will clearly demonstrate) more than adequate for you to provide an effective integration of technology into your classroom. If you have one or two computers and some other teacher nearby has two, learn how to plan computer use times jointly on occasion, so that both of you can try things that are possible when more than one computer is available within a single classroom.

Case Study ▬

Revolution, One Step At A Time

Jessica Wright, a high school mathematics teacher, gradually created a new classroom environment through her own personal "computer revolution." Her story tells how, with only three computers, she gradually was able to:

- provide concrete and immediate visual images and representations to math concepts,
- develop a new vision of education which integrated NCTM standards with computer technology,
- use classroom technology as an effective instrument for curriculum improvement.

With the new National Council of Teachers of Mathematics (NCTM) standards looming before her, Jessica Wright enrolled in a "Computers and Mathematics" course offered by a local college. Although she was aware of the NCTM standards, she learned about them in greater depth as she explored a variety of comprehensive pieces of software for teaching and learning math. Among these were *Algebra Xpresser*, *3D Images*, *Geometer's Sketchpad*, and *Geo-Explorer*. These inquiry-based materials would become the keys she would use to unlock her traditional classroom.

As she gained confidence with the technology, Jessica gradually began to introduce it to the classroom. Algebra I was first. Jessica used the computer and an LCD panel. She gave her usual lecture but took advantage of the software to produce instant graphs. She was able to present concrete and immediate visual images of the math problems. Before long, she noticed how much more attention the students paid to the computer graphs.

Her next small step was allowing her students to use the technology. This was really a two-tiered innovation for her. The first tier was the change in classroom structure. With no chance of getting a math lab, her only option was to use computers in her classroom. With persistent pressure, she secured three of the school's Macintosh computers for "short term" assignment to her room. Even with three computers, she had to plan carefully for how her twenty four students would have access to them. Despite a rash of suggestions for using cooperative learning groups from a variety of sources, she initially avoided that approach.

Initially, Jessica assigned students to the computers six at a time (two per computer), while she taught the rest of the class from the chalkboard. This immediately created problems. The students were more interested in watching their classmates at the computers. "Chalk talk" could not compete with hands-on. So she modified the class and scheduled one computer day a week. This schedule, however, limited students' access to the computers even more.

Finally, Jessica did try cooperative learning. She created small work groups of three to five, and learned facilitation techniques for cooperative learning. Then she had to make assignments fit this new form. Problems had to be complex enough to fully engage three to five students. She was waist deep in curriculum reform.

"I used to work very hard at telling my students about mathematics," Jessica later remarked at a teachers' meeting. "I would constantly think about how to better explain what I taught. Now it's different. I have a new tool for teaching math, the computer. I use this tool to show math as a dynamic visual experience. My students use it as a tool of inquiry to seek answers and ask questions."

Next came the second tier of the process: curriculum change. As students worked at the computer solving "in-context" problems, Jessica began to observe a visual learning element that hadn't been present in her classroom before. Many of her kids seemed to have a talent and preference for manipulating the graphs and other visual elements of math in a manner similar to how she might manipulate the symbols of an equation. The students seemed to have a visual intuition about math, where she seemed to have more of a symbolic intuition.

This new access to instant visualizations sparked the kids to learn much more. Their questions centered on the pictorial display, not on the algebraic operations. Armed with this new insight, Jessica retooled her curriculum yet again: First teach the graphs, then the operations. The students responded to her new approach, and many undeniably improved.

For Jessica Wright and her students, mathematics had been transformed, slowly. Now the curriculum, the methods, and the technology all seemed to work in "sync," and together provided a springboard for student learning.

"Most teachers will utilize new technologies only to the degree that they believe that these technologies will help them solve problems that they define as important"

Understanding the Context

Dear Dr. DeLeet:

    I am the mild-mannered principal of a large metropolitan middle school. I am the very model of a modern instructional leader, but I have to confess to you that there is no way that I seem able to get my teachers (who are all wonderful, highly-motivated, and sincere people) to use all these expensive computers we've bought. Oh, sure, they occasionally let the kids go play with *Math Blaster* after they've finished their *real* work, but I sure don't see us getting much bang for our bucks. I'd like to help them do more, but I don't know much about computers myself, and, frankly, I don't want to get the teachers angry at me by making unreasonable demands. My question is: What's reasonable?

                    Clark K, A.B.D.

Barriers to Integration

- **To key or not to key; that is the question.**
- **Is there no fuel like an old fuel?**
- **Out of sight, out of sync?**

When Adelaide Smith heard she could get two computers for her classroom, as part of a state, "whole school" Chapter I program, she was quick to volunteer. Adelaide always tried to get the latest and greatest equipment for her students.

When her computers arrived at the beginning of the year, she did what she had seen lots of teachers do. She stuck them out in the corridor, and used them to reward students who finished their real work early, by letting them go out and play computer games. Then a funny thing happened. Unbeknownst to Adelaide, the Chapter I people expected her to use the new computers inside her classroom. Even more astonishing, they expected her to integrate them in the math lessons she taught, and even to make sure that the Chapter I students in her class especially benefited from their use. When Adelaide finally understood these conditions, she quickly withdrew from the project. Didn't these people understand? She had no idea how to integrate these blinking monsters in classroom lessons; nobody had even let her know that that was possible. She had no idea how to organize cooperative learning groups around a computer, and she wasn't all that certain that it was even such a good idea. "Oh, well" she thought, "good riddance to new rubbish."

Why are there so many classroom teachers who still make little or no use of computers in their classrooms? Even *TIME* magazine acknowledges (April 20, 1991) that the impact of technology on the basic operations of most classrooms is "practically nil." What accounts for this inertia?

A Few Theories

One explanation can be based on M.A. Cosden's findings that elementary school teachers overwhelmingly believe that mastery of basic skills is the major benefit of computer use, and that they associate the accomplishment of that goal with drill and practice computer activities. So for the kind of teacher who would be motivated by the other more exciting and more engaging benefits of classroom computer use, the real payoffs are not always apparent. (*Journal of Special Education*, 1988, p. 242-253.)

Another theory, espoused by Larry Cuban, holds that the introduction of new technologies into classrooms in any broad-based way always comes into direct conflict with "the ways schools are currently structured." Asking teachers to risk what seemingly works by trying to meet expectations that are "out of sync" with their organizational realities goes well beyond what "most ordinary, well-intentioned, people" can do. So despite the heroic efforts of the few, who prove what is possible, expecting similar behavior from the many, who work under over-whelming restraints, is unrealistic. Embedded in school organizations are entrenched beliefs about the nature of knowledge, how students learn, and how teachers should teach. These beliefs reshape new technologies to "fit the contours of the setting" and, in so doing, sap their potency. (*Teachers and Machines*, 1986.)

In a similar but more pointed explanation, Seymour Papert, in *The Children's Machine*, traces the erratic history of computers in schools as an exercise in "neutralizing a subversive instrument." In the early 1980's, he maintains, the few computers in school ended up in the classrooms of teachers who showed the greatest enthusiasm. But as computers proliferated, "the administrators moved in" and put all the computers in one room, so students could come together and study computers for an hour a week. By "inexorable logic," the next step was to introduce a curriculum for the computer.

Thus was the computer defined as a new subject. Instead of "changing the emphasis from impersonal curriculum to excited live exploration" by students, the computer became used for reinforcing "standard hierarchical thinking." What had started as an instrument of change was neutralized by the system and converted into "an instrument of consolidation." Papert calls the development of these "misleadingly named" computer labs "a kind of immune response to a foreign body." The logic of the process was to bring the intruding computer "back into line" with the ways of the school.

More Barriers

The barriers that Cosden, Cuban, and Papert describe are real; other, equally plausible, explanations have also been advanced:

- ◆ Those classroom teachers most likely to introduce significant change aren't aware of the most exciting and interesting pedagogical payoffs.
- ◆ The leading manufacturers of hardware and software have aided and abetted the schools' journey down the primrose path of computer marginality, because that path provides the most immediate opening for their products.

◆ Instructional leaders (for example, principals)are not sufficiently aware of the potential value of a few, well-used classroom computers in meeting their most valued instructional objectives.

◆ Too few instructional leaders are aware of available, systematic mechanisms by which *school-wide* classroom computer use can successfully be introduced.

◆ Models of how to deploy effectively the number of computers practically available per classroom (i.e., two or three), though they exist, are not readily available.

◆ Quality standards for separating the wheat from the chaff of classroom computer usage are not readily available.

◆ Nobody has a clear fix on what computers are for, so they are used for this and that, with no sharp vision of their central purpose.

◆ Until very recently, there was not enough exciting, motivating, easy-to-use software to support effective use of computers at every level in every subject.

◆ Many older teachers were never exposed to computers when they were learning to become teachers.

Even among teachers with significant computer experience, Bank Street College of Education researchers found that the majority of the top barriers of the past remain among the top barriers today. Teachers report not having enough time to prepare computer-based lessons, nor enough time in the schedule to include computer-based instruction. They have problems scheduling enough computer time for various classes. Two administrative barriers (help in supervising computer use and financial support) now also figure centrally for these teachers. Apparently, many teachers, although in comparatively advantaged situations with respect to technology, continue to experience the integration of computers into their schools as a struggle for support. (Hawkins and Sheingold, in Culbertson, et.al., *Microcomputers and Education*, 1986.)

Barriers Away

How, then, can we get around these barriers?

◆ On the one hand, we can work on each barrier individually.

◆ We can find ways to make available successful models of classroom integration of computers to teachers and educational leaders as a whole.

◆ We can include instruction in the use of computers in teacher-
training programs.

◆ On the other hand, some of these barriers may dissolve over time, as
younger, more computer-literate teachers enter the work-force and
more and more communities buy more and more hardware.

In the end, however, before most teachers, or principals, are likely to take
the time, energy, and effort required to learn about effective uses of computers
within classrooms, they need to know whether it is worth it.   Most teachers will
utilize new technologies only to the degree that they believe that these technologies will help them solve problems that *they* define as important. And they
must be convinced that it won't take some tremendous expenditure of blood,
sweat, and tears to learn how to use them.

Knocking Down the Barriers

• **How can you start spreading the news?**
• **Are you manning barricades that don't exist?**
• **Do as I say, not as I do?**

*Veronica Gilbey is a eighth-grade teacher in Denver. Computers have long been a
part of her teaching life. But in the past two years, a new program in her school has radi-
cally altered her vision of what computers are for. Before she became a part of the
Computer Integration and Cooperation Program, Veronica bought into a lot of the conventional wisdom regarding computer usage: "The computer is a great drill and practice tool
for slow learners. It is a good motivating reward for when students finish their work early.
Kids need to get computer literacy skills before they get to high school." Then along came
CICP, with its alternative vision: training the eighth graders as computer tutors of children in the sixth-grade class downstairs, putting them in cooperative learning groups
around the computer, using computers as a basic tool to teach all the core subjects eighth
graders have to learn. Veronica now sees a startling difference in what computers can do
for teachers: "I used to think of them as just another audio-visual aid to bring in as an
extra, but now I realize that they are valuable tools of my trade that provide an important
alternative way to help children learn the basic stuff we have to teach," she says.*

The first step in getting rid of barriers is to get a better sense of what those
barriers are. You have limited ability to break down some of these barriers, but

what you can do first is to conceptualize and envision alternatives. Knocking down your own mental and intellectual barriers is as important as increasing the funding of new hardware and more useful software.

Preaching to the Choir

The existence of a core group of computer users in education may make it harder rather than easier to get the rest of the educational community involved. Many articles, books, classroom teaching suggestions, et. al., assume that EVERYBODY can deal with what only this core group understands.

One way to involve the rest is to provide teachers with computer integration ideas and materials that:

a.   address core curriculum issues that are important to THEM,

b.   are relatively easy to implement with limited resources,

c.   go well beyond drill and practice to use methods that good teachers can respect.

Teaching the Teachers

While we have to figure out easy and successful ways to ease teachers who have not used computers into the use of technology, we do not need to hesitate or shrink back from requiring them to learn these new skills. None of us would

use a car mechanic who was unfamiliar with the new electronics that have been introduced into automobiles in the past decade, and we would certainly expect our dentists to have upgraded their tools to meet the changing hygienic standards in their fields. Parents have at least as much right to expect their children's teachers to keep up with the new tools of their trade that can make a crucial difference in the success of the educational enterprise.

Pre-service education programs have to start prioritizing. We must start making intelligent decisions about what to teach the teachers of the twenty-first century about computer use. Pre-service teacher education programs must show prospective teachers how to actually use computers as a tool of their future trade. The first priority should be teaching teachers how to integrate the computer as a useful teaching tool, and the best way to do that, by far, is by example. Teachers of teachers will need to use computers as tools in their teaching before their students can realistically be expected to go out into the field and integrate computers into their own work.

Computers and the Central Focus

The attitude that computers in the classroom are an "extra" creates a mental barrier on the part of overtaxed teachers, who have "important" things to accomplish. Linking computer use to those important things is key to both the quantity and quality of future classroom computer use.

Teacher training must demonstrate in convincing fashion that computers can help relieve the pressure on classroom teachers rather than add to it. To do so requires tying computers to the important, key tasks of classroom instructors, such as learning to solve math word problems, answering comprehension questions about a paragraph, writing a clear business letter, carrying out scientific inquiry, and so forth.

Changing the Decision Makers

Teachers need to have more say about how computers are used in their schools. Principals need to realize that they cannot cede decision-making power over what goes on with computers in their schools to some system-wide computer guru whose main efforts have helped keep most ordinary classroom teachers isolated from meaningful computer use. Principals must understand not just that in-classroom computers *can* make a big difference in the instructional practices of their classrooms, but that they *should already* be making a difference. Even principals who believe in the importance of their roles as instructional leaders are usually not particularly interested in how computers are used in their schools, because they have not yet made the connection between in-classroom computers and instructional leadership. Helping your principal recognize these needs may require some assertion on your part.

Provide a Clear Vision

In many respects, the biggest problem teachers probably face in overcoming the barriers to using computers in the classroom is a lack of vision. To remove the barriers to effective computer use in the classroom, you, your school, or your school system must have a coherent and forceful vision of how computers can be used. This book presents a vision that involves using computers in your classroom to support the central focus of instruction, using software that supports a variety of learning styles and cooperative learning. It is intended to help you develop your own personal vision as the necessary first step.

Integrating Students with Special Needs

- **Is separate inherently unequal?**
- **How can we provide power to the powerless?**
- **What is so special?**

CompuCID (Computer Classroom Integration Demonstration, pronounced Komp-u-kid) pioneered new ways to use technology as a tool to integrate children with special needs in regular classrooms. The CompuCID project: (1) trained teachers to use computers to integrate children with special needs into regular classrooms; (2) trained teachers in how to use the computer as a part of innovative approaches to learning (e.g., cooperative learning); (3) trained teachers (K-8) in how to use the computer as a classroom tool to pursue major objectives of the regular curriculum; and (4) showed teachers how to implement peer tutoring and cross-age tutoring activities around the computer. A manual on implementing this model has been prepared for dissemination by the Foundation for Technology Access in Richmond, California.

The CompuCID project remains an exception to the way most schools utilize computers with their students with special needs. Most descriptions of the use of computers in schools claim that special educators have learned to make more significant use of computers than their regular education counter-parts. They acknowledge that special educators are making a greater effort than most other educators to take advantage of the new educational possibilities created by computers.   What they do not acknowledge as readily is that what these schools do with their computers often does not really make much sense.

Problems and Problem Areas

In many school situations, the use of the computer with students with special needs is at best a double-edged sword.   It may provide the students with greater access to learning certain subjects, but only at the (totally unnecessary) expense of increasing, rather than decreasing, the likelihood that the student with special needs will learn in a segregated setting.   Most special educators need to learn how to use the computer specifically as an *integration* tool.   Most regular classroom teachers need to know more about how to collaborate successfully with special needs teachers within the regular classroom.

When schools use computers with students with special needs, they far too often utilize them as one-on-one instruments for rote or drill-and-practice learning.   This belies two important realities: (a) that such students can benefit more from computer activities that involve learning cooperatively with co-learners, and (b) that computer activities that go beyond drill-and-practice have a more valuable effect on their learning.   The computer is also a very important potential socialization tool for students with certain kinds of disabilities.   It can help them communicate more easily, more comfortably, and more clearly; facilitate their independence; and help raise their confidence in social situations.

When special educators use computers with students with special needs, only rarely does their work indicate their understanding of how computers (especially the Macintosh computer) can be used as a scaffold to the regular curriculum from which students with special needs are often excluded.   For many students with learning disabilities, just the simple ability to use a word processor for writing tasks can make school a vastly more pleasant and successful experience.   The computer can facilitate having students with special needs tutor others; being a tutor can prove an invaluable experience in breaking self-stereotypes, and stereotyping by others.

Finally, special educators rarely take full advantage of the possibilities inherent in parent-assisted-learning with respect to computers, or of the potential contribution of siblings in the learning of students with special needs. Computers are still (erroneously) viewed as such daunting instruments that few educators see how willing and able parents, older siblings, and even younger siblings might be a part of the computer-assisted learning picture.

Realizing the Potential

Luckily, there has also been a great deal of successful practice. Below are listed a number of ideas for successful computer classrooms, ideas suggested by teachers with special needs students:

1. Begin with a fundamental belief in the purpose and goals of mainstreaming, and maintain high expectations for all students.
2. Arrange the classroom so that it lends itself to a variety of instructional strategies (direct instruction, cooperative learning, individualized learning tasks).
3. Create a climate for acceptance of experimentation by students and teacher; regard mistakes as learning opportunities.

4. Write lesson plans which focus on problem solving and the process of learning, in addition to the curriculum content.
5. Solicit administrative understanding of mainstreaming goals and assistance in creating resources to deal with the demands that mainstreaming places on classroom teachers.

6. Involve the parents of regular and special education students.
7. Clearly state goals for student achievement; allow opportunities for every student to succeed.

The Computer and Inequality

- **Do poor schools teach to type, not to think?**
- **Why is it that the more things change, the more they remain unequal?**
- **To each according to his/her (special) needs.**

In an inner-city school in Milwaukee, students troop down to the Computer Laboratory, to get the only computer exposure they will get during the day. They line up, each staring at a different "dumb" computer monitor. What is in the computer is controlled "downtown," by a central computer administering a networked basic skills program that records the students' achievement progress as they plod through the skill programs.

In affluent schools, students more often get to use computers for creative exploration and higher-order thinking tasks. Teachers in poorer districts concentrate on drill and practice routines for reading, writing, and arithmetic.

Providing equitable distribution of computer resources is one of our biggest challenges. Concerned that the new technologies are widening the gap between the haves and the have-nots, educational policy-makers find themselves with a brand new set of difficult decisions to make. Major problems center on equitable treatment for low-income students, for girls as well as boys, and for low-achieving as well as academically able students. Ironically, like so many educational technologies and innovations preceding it, the microcomputer raised expectations for greater equity and quality in education. Unfortunately, for most school districts, the issues of quality and equity remain largely unresolved.

Economic Inequities

The imbalance in computer resources for rich and poor students is an obvious and pressing aspect of the equity issue. Students with computers at home start with a considerable advantage, an advantage not available to low-income students. Special funding programs and monetary gifts for computer equipment often compound the problem, since the pressure for the use of computers comes mainly from predominantly middle-class parents, who want the district to help their children master the computer.

Achievement Inequities

Differences in the computer instruction offered to students of varying abilities often parallel those described for low- and middle-income students. In many districts, programming courses are provided for students "good in math" and computer-assisted instruction are offered to "disabled learners." In some cases, the vast middle range of students have no contact at all with computers. The educational assumptions behind such ability-stratified usage patterns and the likely educational outcomes need careful examination if these kinds of inequities are to be eliminated. Even when principals in poor schools try to integrate computers more creatively, their plans often fall prey to the following logic of survival. There is enormous pressure to raise standardized test scores. And, paradoxically, rote computer-based training can increase scores by a few points, even while it deadens critical thinking.

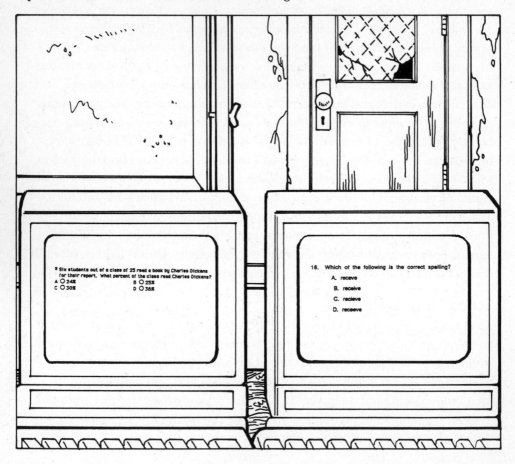

Gender Inequities

Do female students get equal access and exposure to computer opportunities in school settings? Unless teachers are careful, subtle kinds of gender discrimination can emerge. Some observers suggest, for example, that boys gravitate to computers more readily than girls because they are greater risk takers, and thereby "elbow" the girls away from these scarce resources. Others question the kind of gender biases that creep into the software produced by (mostly male) computer programmers.

This book tries to help classroom teachers cope with this issue within the broader context of learning how to exploit the tremendous potential that computers have in helping to accommodate the many differences in learning styles that they confront in any classroom. Basic gender differences and differing acculturation patterns doubtless represent important influences on the learning styles of children well before they reach school age, but schools can reinforce or counteract inequities. Teachers can turn the computer into an important ally in coping with differences.

The Problem Inequities Create

If personal computers fulfill their potential to increase learning, the education gap between learners in the more advantaged strata and those who do not have access to the personal computer will increase. Higher-income learners will become more competent learners and, to the extent that this increases productivity, their income advantage will increase.

One way to deal with computer equity is for local and state officials to press for federal legislation that provides greatly increased funds for poor school systems to train teacher and parents, to make school use more effective and encourage home-borrowing programs. For individual classroom teachers of educationally disadvantaged students, the message is clear: use computers in ways that help students gain control of computers as instruments of higher-order thinking skills, not to prepare them for low-wage jobs operating electronic cash registers or bar codes.

Case Study ■

An Off Week

This case describes how a secondary school math department attempted to resolve differences in attitudes about the value of computer instruction among its members. During a week's "vacation" from their teaching responsibilities, two members of the department were able to visit a neighboring school and see how teachers there:

- used a few pieces of exceptional software to get their students more deeply engaged in math concepts that often appear dry and distant to most kids,
- thoroughly integrated computer technology into their everyday teaching assignments.

Paul King was tired of the debate within the department. He thought, "We always divide into two camps: those who feel that computer algebra will cause students' skills to atrophy or inhibit their development, and those who believe, as I do, that the computer will improve students' conceptual understanding."

After the meeting he approached his department head: "Tom, our discussions are not going to convert anyone. I think it might be more productive if we visited other schools and could see first hand what a computer actually can do for the teaching of mathematics."

Paul visited an Algebra 2 class that was beginning to study quadratic equations. What struck him immediately was how the teacher, Harvey Collins, first motivated his class by presenting problem situations for which quadratic equations are useful: projectile motion, revenue, profit/demand/cost functions, and fitting rules to curvilinear data. Collins prepared dynamic demonstrations using *The Geometer's Sketchpad*, *MathCad*, and *Excel*.

The first strategy was guess-and-test successive approximation. The students were asked to obtain some possible solutions with a calculator. Then they used a spreadsheet program in which they entered input values and rules to generate the output. Students played with the step increments for input values, to refine their search for a better approximation to the solution. This guess and test strategy, now feasible with the tedium of the calculation being handled through technology, really strengthened their skills in reading and interpreting data. This approach also emphasizes a functional viewpoint which is a unifying mathematical concept. With an appreciation and understanding from the table, they then graphed the function, using *GraphWiz*. By adjusting the axes, the domain and range, students could zoom in on the solutions and the regions they wished to explore.

As the week progressed, Collins presented a more formal analysis of solutions to the quadratic related to number and type of roots, and formal algebraic manipulation (such as factoring and the quadratic formula). The kids felt that they had a variety of tools that enabled them to test their intuition.

While Paul was not surprised at all at what he had seen and heard, he was anxious to hear from Diane about her week. On the first day Diane had entered the class with skepticism. Her sponsoring teacher, John, had previously explained that they were going to use a simulation game called *SimCity* to develop and deepen an understanding of the concepts of variable and function, and the cause-and-effects relations they represent. *SimCity* makes the user Mayor and City Planner. The user is given a set of rules on city planning and management, and tools to plan, lay out, zone, build, bulldoze, and manage a city. The challenge the game provides is to figure out how the system (i.e., the city) works, and to take control of it. Depending on the mayor's choices and design skills, simulated citizens move in or out in search of a better life. Real-time graphs, demographic maps, budget windows, and opinion polls guide the decision-makers.

Diane admitted to Paul that at first she was turned off by the notion of using a game at the high school level. But she saw how this simulation engaged the kids in a thoughtful, meaningful way across disciplines, and how it required that they acquire and apply skills to real-life problems. Paul was pleased that Diane was just as excited as he was by the potential impact computers offered. They knew they had a lot to learn, and not just about the hardware and software (that seemed like the easier part). Once you've got the tools, how can you use them to their best advantage to create a meaningful impact on curriculum and instructional practices? From their visits, they knew it could be done, and they were now willing to give it a try.

"MAYBE YOU KIDS WOULD LIKE TO
WORK ON THIS PROJECT TOGETHER."

"In addition, frequently the most desirable way to use software that goes beyond drill and practice is in cooperative groups, which can add the documented benefits of cooperative learning to active learning and skill development."

Demystifying the Obvious

Dear Dr. DeLeet:

I'm in my first year of teaching and, I swear, just getting middle school kids to sit still and listen for ten minutes takes all the energy I can muster. Now my two new Macs have arrived, and the curriculum coordinator has just dropped by with a list of available software and a clear "message" that I am to have the Macs up and running in my classroom throughout the school day. I got some computer literacy skills on the IBMs at college, but they never showed use how to use computers inside classrooms. I don't even know whether any of this software is any good. My questions are: How do I pick the right software (without adding to the stress I'm already feeling)? And then, what do I do with it?

Abandoned in Stressville

CHAPTER 4

Software: the Varieties of Choice

- **How can you keep your eyes on the prize (winners)?**
- **Why AREN'T the best things in life free?**
- **How can simple be powerful?**

Audry had a quick decision to make. Transferred to a new school over the summer, she was delighted to find that her principal had allocated $450 for software for her ninth-grade math class. But she had to decide what to buy within the first two weeks in September, long before she could get to know her new school or her new students. What to do?

How can an ordinary classroom teacher separate the software wheat from the software chaff? Winners of major software awards from publications like *Technology and Learning, Electronic Learning,* and *Media and Methods* help provide some guarantees, but not all of these meet the standards discussed in this book.

There are three major sources of software, each with its advantages and disadvantages. You can buy software directly from publishers, who exhibit at conferences and advertise in magazines. Many publishers offer 30-day trials of their software. Publishers also develop reputations for their entire product line. As a rule, you will probably have luck with software from a publisher with a reputation for quality products, like *Wings, Toucan,* or *Scholastic.*

Most schools buy from dealers or distributors, who sell software from many different publishers and rarely market their own. The main advantage is that you can buy software from many different publishers from one company, using one purchase order. Look for a dealer with a 30-day trial period.

You can buy software from stores, which sometimes even have computers running software, allowing you to try out possible purchases. Many stores, however, do not allow you to return software. And beware salespeople. Many are primarily interested in selling whatever is easiest, and certainly whatever they have in stock. Many salespeople know little about the few educational products they do carry, and they know nothing about the thousands of titles they do not carry. *Caveat Emptor.*

Software Categories

Thinking about software according to categories can be useful–for example, to compare two pieces of simulation software rather than to compare a simulation product with an educational game. Sometimes it makes sense to select a particular piece of software because of the kind it is. What follows is a brief discussion of some of the major categories of educational software.

(1) Drill-and-Practice

This is still one of the most common forms of educational software. It is based primarily on rote learning and repetition. This book avoids D&P software, because it fails to exploit some of the biggest advantages of computers, and is of extremely limited utility.

(2) Tutorials

Educational tutorials tend to be straightforward instructional products. The best tutorials take advantage of some of the special characteristics of the computer: experiments, animations, demonstrations, simulations, rich feedback, and so forth.

(3) Educational Games

Educational games are designed to combine the fun of games with the information needed in an educational product.

(4) Tool-based Learning

In educational settings, software "tools" usually refer to the major productivity tools: word processors, spreadsheets, database programs, and graphing programs. Tool-based learning products use these productivity tools to teach regular content, such as science, language arts, math, and social studies.

(5) Simulations

One of the powers of the computer is its ability to simulate real-life experiences and give students variables over which they exercise control. Educational simulations can be text-only, or include graphics.

(6) Problem-solving Software

Among the first examples of quality educational software was general problem-solving software, which allows students to focus on problem-solving skills as such. Some problem-solving software now also fits specific school content, especially science, math, and social studies.

(7) Educational Adventures

Educational adventures combine some of the features of their consumer counterparts (elaborate game-play, finding lost items, making decisions and living with their consequences, gathering items along the way) with the need to use information (often subject-specific) to answer questions to advance in the adventure.

Software Selection Criteria

One criterion to use in selecting software is cost-effectiveness. Cost, per se, is only a part of this issue. Obviously, if you can get a good word processor appropriate for your students for $50 instead of spending $350, the former is more cost-effective. Generally, the real issue with cost-effectiveness is how many students can use the software how many times. If, for example, you can get all of your seventh-grade science students to use an educational adventure one time each for just an hour, and you have one hundred students each year, even a $100 product is quite cost-effective.

In an age of increasingly scarce resources, flexibility and versatility in a single piece of software become an important software selection criterion. One of the things teachers like about certain kinds of software (such as Tom Snyder Productions' *Timeliner*) is that they can get multiple uses at different skill levels out of certain kinds of software. This is especially true for productivity tools or tool-like programs: word processors, database programs, spreadsheets, etc.

A criterion that is more rarely mentioned is how the software fits the kinds of instructional strategies the teacher prefers. Because this book favors peda-gogical strategies that support inquiry, cooperative learning, problem-solving, etc., we have chosen software and classroom activities that lend themselves to such strategies in Part II, which presents practical classroom activities. In select-ing software, you look for consistency between the software and your own instructional strategies of choice.

Finally, many educators talk in terms of a criterion that reflects the power of the computer: interactiveness. Books cannot be interactive, and computer software can be. Therefore, look for software that is truly interactive. What characterizes interaction? Look for software that calls for thoughtful action on the part of students and that provides feedback when they answer questions incorrectly. Look for software that offers your students variables they can control. Look for software which can adjust to different students at different levels of ability (intellectual or computer skill). These are some of the char-acteristics of truly interactive software.

A Word About Shareware

Shareware–public domain software–often (although not always) costs very little money. You may not have to spend more than a few dollars for this software, unless you like it and/or want the printed documentation, at which point you have to/can send in a little more money. Some of this software is quite good, but most of it is, at best, spotty. It is generally not professionally packaged and often not well tested or debugged, and it usually lacks developer support. Just keep those things in mind. On the other hand, the software situation is not as simple as: "You get what you pay for." A lot of commercially-available software at much higher prices is not much better.

Software Serving Two Masters

- **Can you kill two birds with one mouse?**
- **Round up the unusual suspects.**
- **Check your hidden assumptions at the door.**

In the teen movie Pump Up The Volume, *Christian Slater plays a high school student who uses his guerrilla radio station to bring down an unscrupulous high school principal. The principal's crime? Cutting off the school's underachievers from oppor-tunities to stay in school in order to pump up her school's standard achievement test results. Her (erroneous) assumption? That only with high-handed, old-fashioned, hard-nosed drill-and-practice methods could her school preserve its reputation as a "winner." Slater wins his battle under the usual preposterous teen movie circumstances. Yet the film manages to make an interesting educational point: Maybe there is a better way to produce achievement in basic skills.*

This book takes a similar position regarding the choices that you can make with the software you integrate into your teaching: there is a way to use computers to promote the basic skills still overwhelmingly valued in our schools *without* having to resort to dull, drill-and-practice software.

An important prerequisite, however, is the need to check your stereotypes at the door. A key obstacle to realizing what is now possible with computers is the too-common association between increasing achievement levels and using one-on-one, drill-and-practice, basic skill software. This book takes an alternative view: that avoiding drill and practice, using learner-centered software and methods can lead to significant achievement gains–gains that show up on standardized tests. At the same time, doing so will develop the kinds of learning skills that make *future* achievement gains more likely!

In addition, frequently the most desirable way to use software that goes beyond drill and practice is in cooperative groups, which can add the documented benefits of cooperative learning to active learning *and* skill development.

Basic Skills

The definition of what constitutes basic skills is undergoing rapid change. For example, the new standards of the National Council of Teachers of Mathematics emphasize that students should work with "real-world related" problems in mathematics lessons. A software simulation, for example, can provide students with a motivating format for running a small business, stock an inventory, and determine a selling price for their product. Solving word problems is also a focus of the NCTM standards. Learning to *write* math word problems may do more for the development of problem-solving ability than tackling math word problems alone. Activities that allow students to create a survey and then graph the results, or enable students at the elementary level to develop a sense of geometry can help them to more easily advance to higher mathematics. The mathematical skills necessary for students in the twenty-first century will also emphasize working collaboratively in groups to solve problems, using technology as tools in this process.

Software Alternatives

A number of different kinds of "electronic books" illustrate some of the ways that software can promote active learning and maximize student achievement. Software products like *Just Grandma and Me* and the "Discis Series" are designed to help students develop reading skills and fluency. Such programs can read the story to the students as they highlight the words. Students can click on words to get definitions. Most of these programs have animated illustrations, and many allow students to interact with the book in a variety of ways. Such programs hold promise as alternative ways to "teach" basic reading and code breaking skills.

Even elemental software tools like word processing programs can promote basic skill without resorting to drill-and-practice methods. A number of word processors on the Macintosh, for example, can function as reading as well as writing tools. Many such programs allow students complete freedom to write (active learning) and then can read what is on the screen back to the student.

A Concrete Example

More and more, school-based projects are being explicitly designed to insure that the software they involve will serve these two masters. The Teacher-Led Computer (TLC) Project in Arlington, Massachusetts set out to do precisely that. Classroom teachers use software that teaches reading comprehension, solving math word problems, writing about science, and following scientific method, among other skills. TLC trains classroom teachers to integrate computers into their day-to-day classroom work, in a way that has a direct impact on the improvement of students' achievement scores, without recourse to drill-and-practice software.

The project's goals focus on

(1) promoting achievement gains,

(2) enhancing students' ability to think for themselves, and

(3) helping teachers learn how to combine cooperative learning techniques with computer technology.

Such practices suggest that basic skills enhancement is not just a legitimate goal, but a very desirable goal, *when linked* to exciting instructional methods and appropriate ways of evaluating accomplishment of the achievement goals. Assume a software tool exists that will help you teach the content in the way you want to teach it. Then develop the software finding skills to "round up the unusual suspects." Finally integrate learner-centered software with skill-building classroom activities.

Multi-Media Alternatives

- **Do you have to walk the walk before you talk the talk?**
- **The future isn't what it used to be.**
- **The more the merrier?**

(1) In a suburban school outside of Detroit, eighth-grade science teachers spend the first 20 minutes every Monday, Wednesday, and Friday introducing science concepts through the "magic" of interactive videodisc. Then the machines are shut off, science classes go back to the "status quo ante media," and no other teachers in the school get to touch the new multi-media equipment.

(2) A team of sixth-grade students sits at a computer connected to a videodisc player and completes a series of "interactive" lessons, keyboarding answers as the program progresses. While the students are focused on the solution of a dastardly environmental crime, they are learning important information about the eco-structure of the shore, solving math "word problems," and solving a mystery closely related to the ecology curriculum mandated for their grade. When they finish, they start a non-computer activity involving

analysis of the school's drinking water, while a new team uses the interactive video equip-
ment to participate in an adventure involving math word problems.

These two stories illustrate the pitfalls and potential of multi-media materials. When multi-media materials are used outside the boundaries of the regular
classroom curriculum, their use is severely limited and may not justify their
expense. On the other hand, when they are thoroughly integrated into the
core curriculum of a regular classroom, they can offer exciting ways to engage
the attention and various intelligences of a wide variety of students.

What is Multi-Media

So, what exactly is "multi-media," this wave of the future that already exists, in a
fashion? As with so many new phenomena, there is no precise definition. Put
most simply, multi-media products combine video, audio, textual, and graphic
material. These materials typically require a hardware configuration that
combines a computer with a videotape player, an audiotape player, a CD-ROM
player, and/or a video/laser disk player.

Multi-media products have two distinct advantages over computer software products. First, multi-media products usually allow for the storage of vast quantities of information (both text and visuals). CD-ROM platters and videodiscs hold immense amounts of information compared even to typical computer hard drives, let alone floppy disks. Thus, these products can put vast amounts of information at teachers' and students' fingertips.

Second, multi-media products tend to be highly visual, because multi-media hardware can store so much information, including high resolution color photographs and video. Thus, multi-media products look and feel much more like television than like typical computer software.

What are the Problems?

Until very recently, one big problem with multi-media was analogous to the problem educational software as a whole had during much of the 1980's: the lack of high quality material to fit the existing curriculum. As a result, most people using it used it for extras and enrichment, rather than in a truly integrative fashion. Although this situation will change over time, keep in mind that lack of quality material still defines most educational software. As a multi-media problem, it will continue even longer.

A second key problem with implementing multi-media materials is its costs and perceived benefits. Costs for equipment and multi-media materials are still relatively high. Having a computer simply is not enough; you must add a CD-ROM drive, a VCR, or a videodisc player. And multi-media software can cost from 2-3 to even 4-5 times the cost of computer software (although costs are falling). Until people perceive benefits to justify this cost, multi-media will be at a disadvantage compared to computer software.

And the Advantages?

One advantage of multi-media activities is their ability to help make the abstract concrete. For example, in *Jasper Woodbury*, students watch Jasper and his friends encounter real-life problems that must be solved by using math skills. Research shows positive effects on problem-posing, problem-solving, and student attitudes towards math. Students can deal with important math topics like decimals, fractions, geometry, measurement, estimation, and statistics within exciting, highly-visual, real-world situations.

Multi-media also can fill in some missing needs for visual learners, who are often at a disadvantage the way schools usually teach. Multi-media makes possible actually showing your students things that you could previously only talk about. Multi-media has the potential to help schools meet new mandates to relate classroom activity to the variety of intelligences that every student brings learning situations, and to adjust to the growing number of students who do not thrive on the highly linguistic, logical-mathematical learning model that dominates most classrooms.

A big future advantage of multi-media is teacher empowerment. Multi-media can let you pick and choose, from among a much wider variety of options, what information you want to present your students. A parallel advantage for students may be the non-linear feeling of control and ownership it may give them. The potential of multi-media is tremendous, but the practical realities inhibiting that potential (small amount of product, unusually high development cost, high acquisition costs, limited perceived value) are, for the moment, even greater. It will justify the cost only AFTER multi-media products exist that:

(1) fit easily and snugly into the regular curriculum that teachers are under the gun to teach,
(2) clearly support student achievement gains, for teachers who are under pressure to promote them,
(3) support the kinds of active learning styles that innovative teachers (who are the ones more likely to buy into technology in the first place) seek,
(4) help classrooms adjust to the needs of mainstreamed students with learning disabilities and differences, and
(5) offer teachers sufficient flexibility and multiple uses to justify the extra cost of the materials.

Computer Hardware

- **If you've seen one, have you really seen 'em all?**
- **Why do you gotta play the hand that's dealt?**
- **All computers are equal, but are some more equal than others?**

Bill Hardy was the new kid on the block, but he was ready to attack his first teaching assignment with all the new knowledge at his command. His college professors had prepared him for the math classroom of tomorrow; he knew how to deal with interactive

video, CD-Rom, MTV, VCR, RCA, Hypercard, and even Hyperventilation. But wait,
one lousy Apple IIE? This was not what he expected.

The fundamental hardware question used to be: What computer do we
buy? That is clearly an important question still, particularly for administrators
and computer coordinators charged with purchasing hardware for their school
systems. But the development of educational software has now reached a point
where the fundamental hardware question for you is: How do I get the most
out of what is available?

Today there are hundreds of thousands of computers in American
schools. Whereas in the early 1980s, there were more brands than anyone
wished, the current trends are:

(1) The Macintosh has replaced the Apple IIE and the IIGS as the Apple
computer of choice for school systems.

(2) Secondary schools get new IBMs (or clones) and Macs.

(3) The elementary schools still have more old Apples than anything else.

As a result, you cannot use the excuse that you have got the wrong
computer anymore. Some computers may be better than others, but there is
some good software available for all these machines, and it is worth learning
how to get the most out of the one that you happen to have access to.

If You Can Buy

Although this book is a practical guide for teachers who do not usually get a
chance to choose their computer hardware, teachers are sometimes able to
influence new computer acquisitions. When buying new machines, school
systems need to start making hardware choices with a greater eye towards ease
of use for the technological neophyte.

The most obvious example is the Apple Macintosh, the "computer for the
rest of us" that, for most users, is easier to begin on and easier to use than
either the Apple II or the IBM. The Macintosh also has specific advantages for
children with disabilities. Used with the right utilities (e.g. ACTA), spell-
checkers (e.g., MacWrite II, which catches phonetic misspellings), etc., it can
make writing activities far more pleasant and reinforcing for a large group of
children formerly alienated from this task. Especially for the older, experienced teachers who have not yet integrated computers in their classroom
teaching (i.e., most of the classroom teachers in the country), ease of initial use
can have a profound effect on reinforcing or diffusing unspoken stereotypes
about whether technology is worth bothering with.

Hardware Makes Hardware Easy

In the early days of educational computing, teachers had so many kinds of computers available for purchase that they hardly knew where to begin: Apple II+, Apple IIe, Apple IIc, IBM-PC, IBM-PC AT, Tandy, TI 99/4A, TRS-80, Commodore 64, Commodore 128, Atari, Sinclair, MSX, and on and on. Now the choices are MS-DOS and Mac.

Another factor inhibiting the integration of computers in classrooms is the noise from a dot matrix printer. For some teachers, the noise these printers generate seems overly intrusive and disruptive of the kind of learning environments they want. The advent of the relatively inexpensive laser, or ink jet, printer can eliminate this concern.

Software Makes Hardware Easy

Interestingly enough, one way to make computers less threatening relates to the software that accompanies them. We have to stop thinking that programs like AppleWorks and the Apple IIGS are easy just because an in-group of 10-15% of the teachers have put in the time and effort needed to master them. To encourage teachers to take risks with computers in their classrooms, it is critical to purchase software that is genuinely easy-to-learn and easy-to-use. Many students may have little trouble learning AppleWorks, but it is surprisingly difficult for many teachers. An example of a less well-known, but noticeably easier-to-learn, piece of software is *MindPlay Works*. It was designed for the same purpose as the more well-known integrated packages, but it was designed specifically with teachers and students in mind.

Case Study ▬

Two Masters, One Goal

This is the two-year tale of Karen Deluca, a middle school mathematics teacher. With the support and cooperation of a colleague, Karen created a "value added" curriculum that solved two different problems. She discovered that:
- computers can help get students excited about figuring things out on their own, and give them a greater sense of themselves as competent problem-solvers,
- learner-centered software can develop the kinds of skills that make future as well as present achievement gains more likely,
- a good computer-supported environment can promote problem-solving skills and basic skills simultaneously.

Two years ago, Karen Deluca began changing her math class. She was concerned that her curriculum was failing too many kids, and felt they needed to be engaged in something more powerful than the current curriculum format. They still needed an approach to learning that allowed them to learn and apply the traditional, basic "mathematics knowledge." At the same time, they needed more extensive exposure to, and practice with, problem-solving. What they *didn't* need was more repetitive drill and practice exercises. As a reasonably experienced computer user, Karen felt that somehow computer technology could play an integral part in a new format.

Karen and a good friend and colleague in the science department decided to work together. Their first effort was a simple scientific survey. The topic was ecology, with a particular focus on recycling. The science class developed the survey; and the math class learned about the statistical process. Both classes participated in the actual interviews. Then the math class, using spreadsheets on the computer, did all the statistical work and created a report for the science class. Although Karen and her friend were pleased with the results, they realized that this was more of a joint venture than an interdisciplinary project.

The breakthrough beyond joint ventures came with the *Voyage of the Mimi* series. This series contains video tapes of a dramatic ocean-going adventure of the ship Mimi. The drama of the adventure provides the fodder for dozens of learning activities. In addition, the series contains software for navigation, games, books and other materials for extended curricular activities. This is a true interdisciplinary program that provides opportunities for in-depth scientific and mathematical investigation.

Starting with the video dramas in *Voyage of the Mimi*, Karen and her colleague began to engage students in in-depth units for investigation. The classes loved it. Then they moved on to the software. Karen and her students particularly liked the game and simulation aspects of the program. To be successful with the activities, students had to apply a variety of interdisciplinary skills, including math skills. For example, in a navigation unit, students had to use basic math skills to obtain scientific knowledge. They learned map skills, longitude, latitude, measuring distance, calculating speed, etc. Then, as they played computer simulation games like Pirates Gold, or Hurricane, they had to apply those skills in order to win. The *Voyage of the Mimi* was a hit. Karen was pleased to see her students on a voyage of discovery of their own.

Next, Karen was was able to secure a program that contained a large data base of information about ozone. The software, *Ozone Depletion Module* (Bradford Discovery Series), challenges students to solve various problems by querying the data just as a professional might.

Students had to decide what data they needed, and then plan how to obtain and present the data just as scientists would. They were given a true subset of scientific data and a powerful tool (the computer) with which to manipulate it. The students were actively solving problems that involved real-life applications. Karen couldn't help but notice their fascination with the subject, and their excitement as they worked with the computer.

Today, Karen continues her odyssey into technology in the classroom. She has pursued learner-centered software and methods that promote basic skills development without resorting to dull drill and practice. The software and methodology she chooses merges the traditions of the basic math curriculum with emerging requirements for problem solving. She is secure in her belief that her curriculum is no longer failing kids. They are learning more by being asked to do more, and having a much better time.

QUALITY TIME

"Teachers around the country have discovered a useful little secret: they can get parents to help them do their job--by sending classroom computers home with learner-centered software over weekends and vacations, by providing the growing number of families who now own computers with loaned software and at-home learning activities, etc."

Exploiting the Computer's Full Value

Dear Dr. DeLeet:

   I teach in a large, inner-city school, in a *very* heterogeneous class-room. Many (most?) of my students seem to have some kind of learning disability or reading disability, but I never had any special training in these areas. What I do have are these three new Macintosh computers, which are better than the one I have at home, and a special program budget to buy a reasonable amount of soft-ware or "peripherals." This may be a one-time opportunity, and I don't want to blow it. My problem is: I don't feel I know enough to make the kinds of decisions I have to make in the next few months. My question is: What's the quickest way to find out what I need to know?

Teaching for America

CHAPTER 5

Cooperative Learning

- **Is cooperative learning and computers a marriage made in heaven?**
- **Why doesn't competition compute?**
- **Can computers cooperate?**

Darrell, a student in an inner-city school in Charlotte, North Carolina, is reporting to his seventh-grade class on the progress his group of five students has made on its computer assignment. "Number One: How carefully did we check? We checked very carefully. Number Two: Did we help each other? We did very good on that. Number Three: Did we encourage each other? Err... that is where we should do a little better next time. Number Four: How well did we teach each other? We did that very good."

One of the biggest misconceptions of the computer is that it is designed for individual use. Clearly, individual use of the computer is important in theory. It is the most important use of the computer in business. But learning as an individual exercise is not always, or even most often, the most appropriate or effective pedagogical strategy.

Benefits of Cooperative Learning

Cooperative learning has become a central pedagogy in many classrooms, for its instructional, social, and emotional benefits. The computer can often be more effective within a cooperative learning environment than within an individual-oriented one. Cooperative learning humanizes the computerby enabling you to incorporate children with widely divergent learning styles and abilities within the same group, especially when used with the right software. That is why this book emphasizes using the computer as an element of cooperative learning.

Research suggests that achievement and problem-solving skills can be increased when students work together around a computer. In one such study, for example, the effects of computer-assisted cooperative, competitive, and individualistic instruction were compared according to skills achievement, student-student interaction, and attitudes. Computer-assisted cooperative learning (1) promoted greater daily achievement, (2) led to more successful problem solving, (3) produced more task-related student-student interaction, and (4) increased the perceived status of female students. (Johnson, *et.al.*, "Comparison...," *American Education Research Journal*, Fall, 1986.)

What is Cooperative Learning?

Cooperative learning is a way of structuring student-student interaction so that:

- ◆ students know they can be successful only if their group is successful,
- ◆ students are accountable for their individual understanding and mastery of whatever is being taught,
- ◆ students receive specific instruction in the social skills necessary for the group to succeed,
- ◆ students have the opportunity to discuss how well their group is working and receive feedback to improve future performance.

Learning in groups on a computer is not synonymous with cooperative learning. Turn-taking that occurs when students share a limited resource like a computer involves a degree of cooperation, and students agree to abide by the rules of sharing, but the learning activity may still focus on the individual.

In cooperative learning, you set up varied opportunities for your students to explore "curricular content" along with other learners. These opportunities make your students co-active manipulators, rather than inactive recipients, of information, concepts, and problems. The key to cooperative learning is interdependence. The members of the group must need one another and have a stake in each other's understanding and success. Cooperative learning reinforces your role as "guide on the side," while the use of carefully selected software assures you of the quality of the content available to your students.

Structuring Cooperative Learning

Much software may be used as easily with small groups as with single individuals. Students can solve problems independently, compare answers, discuss disagreements, explain their respective approaches and solutions, and reach agreement on what to enter into the computer. To structure a cooperative computer activity:

(1) Assign your students to groups of two or more with at least one member who is able to run the computer program and one who is task-oriented. A teacher who takes cooperative learning seriously does not arbitrarily create groups; the composition of cooperative leaning groups is as important as their existence.

(2) Instruct students to alternate roles, such as keyboarder (enters data

once there is agreement within the group), explainer (explains how to work the problem or the rule needed to respond appropriately), and group reporter (Darrell's role in the scenario that began this section).

(3) Provide needed materials. Do not throw students in groups and leave them on their own; as much teacher preparation is needed for cooperative learning groups as for whole-class activities.

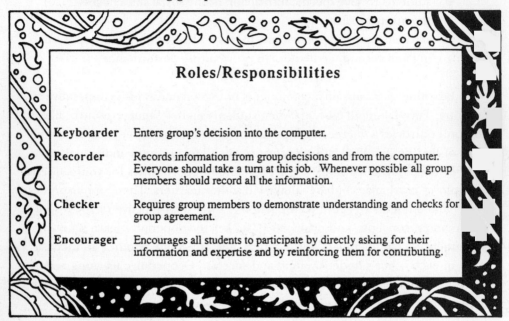

Roles/Responsibilities

Keyboarder   Enters group's decision into the computer.

Recorder   Records information from group decisions and from the computer. Everyone should take a turn at this job. Whenever possible all group members should record all the information.

Checker   Requires group members to demonstrate understanding and checks for group agreement.

Encourager   Encourages all students to participate by directly asking for their information and expertise and by reinforcing them for contributing.

(4) Assign the task of completing a specified number of problems. Students in cooperative learning situations should have as clear and explicit expectations as in any other learning situation.

(5) As a criteria for success structure positive interdependence by requiring students to reach agreement on their responses before entering them into the computer.

(6) Once students have begun, monitor how effectively the groups are working together and fulfilling their role assignments. Students in cooperative learning groups need as much teacher attention as in any other classroom organization.

(7) Ask groups, at the end of the lesson, to discuss briefly how well they worked together and to decide on a behavior they could adopt next time to promote each other's learning. Cooperative learning groups

put students in positions of power and responsibility, and taking as active a part in the evaluation of their own learning as they do in the learning process itself is important.

Advantages for the Teacher

Teachers who have used traditional learning groups find that requiring individual accountability insures that each student contributes to the group. It helps you monitor exactly how much each student has contributed and mastered the target skills. In a cooperative computer activity, for example, each student must be able to explain the activity, produce a printout, or score at a certain level on a quiz. All students must know in advance that they will be responsible individually for demonstrating mastery.

Computers for Accommodating Diversity

- **Why not let a hundred computers bloom?**
- **How is diversity the mother of invention?**
- **Can we think of thinking as a basic skill?**

A computer consultant has been brought in to help "revitalize" a state's thinking about computer use. She began: "I am glad you could all make it to our in-service series. I did not realize there were so many North Carolina teachers interested in using computers as a tool for accommodating the diverse learning styles, levels of learning, and special learning needs of different individuals." Then she offered two examples:

1. Teachers in Tennessee used cooperative learning-by-doing activities around a computer to integrate recently mainstreamed "underachievers" in their classrooms, using math software that simulates math manipulatives.

2. A ninth-grade teacher in Colorado paired students who were her greatest underachievers with her brightest students, and trained them as cross-age computer-tutoring teams, to work with small groups of seventh graders, thus giving the tutors greater self-esteem as well as a way to "learn by teaching."

Then she asked her audience to take a few minutes to think of two more ideas for using the computer to accommodate diversity. [When you've finished this section, think of a couple yourself.]

American classrooms have probably never done a great job of accommodating the diversity of learning styles and abilities in their midst, and now classrooms are getting more diverse just as pressures are growing for raising academic achievement, focusing more on higher order thinking skills, and reducing pullouts of educationally disadvantaged and special needs students. What is a teacher to do?

One clear problem is that contemporary American education too rarely acknowledges, fosters, and takes advantage of the diversity which it increasingly encounters. Some educators even blame their failures on diversity, instead of looking to diversity as a way to increase their success. The computer can provide students with learning disabilities, physical handicaps, or simply previous school failure with fresh entry points for learning and communicating, opportunities never before experienced in schools.

Letting Computers Bloom

An initial approach to using computers to accommodate diversity was to marry Benjamin Bloom's taxonomy of thinking skills with software for computers. Bloom's six thinking skills are:

> (1) knowledge,
> (2) comprehension,
> (3) application,
> (4) analysis,
> (5) synthesis, and
> (6) evaluation.

Each skill is important, but education in many classrooms often ignores "higher-order" skills of analysis, synthesis, and evaluation. To apply technology to remedy this deficiency, some software developers created programs that addressed the development of higher-order thinking. While many drill-based programs reinforce development of lower-order skills, the catalogs of a few publishers (e.g., *Wings* for Learning) are filled with programs to help students learn how to analyze complex situations, create solutions from a synthesis of existing parts, and articulate the thinking processes leading to a solution. But such software is only the beginning of the possibilities.

Multiple Intelligences

Computers provide for a rich variety of teaching strategies, accommodating to widely divergent learning styles and special learning needs. Within a single classroom, they enable you to address all seven intelligences that Howard Gardner has identified in *Frames of Mind*: Linguistic, Logical-Mathematical, Intrapersonal, Spatial, Musical, Bodily-Kinesthetic, and Interpersonal.

Gardner believes that, while each of us may dominate in one of these seven areas, we all have capabilities in the other six. The atmosphere in today's classroom often reinforces the tendency to teach to the linguistic, logical-mathematical, and intrapersonal learner, and virtually to ignore the other four intelligences. Our tendency to teach exclusively to the linguistic, logical-mathematical, and intrapersonal learner has two negative consequences. First, it ignores the needs of the child whose dominant intelligence is not one of these three. Second, it misses the chance to validate and develop the other intelligences in all the children in the room. Time and again we have found that, the more ways a subject is presented, the better the subject is learned and remembered. Gardner's work illuminates a new path for education, one that can do much to help children retain their natural love for learning.

Multiple Intelligences and Computers

How can a teacher use the classroom computer as a tool to meet the needs of a variety of students? How is the teacher to tailor a curriculum to different intelligences? Since the start of the computer revolution, we have been told that this technology would allow the individualization of instruction. Now with Gardner's powerful theory to guide us, we can bring that dream into sharper focus. We can explore the match between the software we have and the dominant intelligence of each child. We can highlight areas for which new software needs to be created and develop specific sets of criteria by which such software can be judged. This focus has been missing in educational computing.

The Rabbit is the Enemy?

- **Is the whole equal to the sum of a bunch of little parts?**
- **Are teacher-proof computers also learning-proof?**
- **If the shoe fits, don't wear it?**

Miriam, a middle school teacher who went through school in the 1950's is pain-fully aware, also, of the criticisms thathigh school teachers are always making of the system's middle school graduates: Kids do not have the faintest idea of what makes a paragraph or even how to string two simple sentences together; they are not prepared for high school math; they cannot spell; they think grammar is Grandpa's wife. Partly as a result, Miriam runs a teacher-led classroom where children put in lots of time learning the basics they have not picked up in theelementary grades. She lets the high achievers do extras, enrichment activities, etc., but the noses of the rest of the children she keeps to the basic skills grindstone. Miriam's questions are: Can a computer help them learn parts of speech? do math word problems? write a clear expository paragraph?

Teachers just starting to use computers inside a classroom, whether veterans like Miriam or beginning teachers, are like customers in a shoe store–they are looking for a comfortable fit. Something that fits their image of what is important to do in a classroom, what is important to learn in that classroom, and how to organize the class to learn it. But they do not know much about all the software choices available to them. It is not "one-size-fits-all" or a "customer is always right" situation. Instead, it's a situation where the universe of choice is limited, with an overwhelming number of choices being made in favor of drill and practice software. Is this good? Bad? Irrelevant?

Why Is a Bunny an Enemy?

In his book, *Insult to Intelligence: The Bureaucratic Invasion of Our Classrooms* (1986), Frank Smith calls *Reader Rabbit*, a best-selling, step-by-step, drill-and-practice package "the enemy." For Smith, the rabbit (and much of the other software used in classrooms) is a symbol of a programmatic approach to instruction that simple-mindedly pretends that children learn by practicing one disjointed systematic piece of learning after another. Children, he contends, cannot learn anything "one fragmented, trivialized, and decontextualized bit at a time." The educational computer industry, he believes, has developed in a way that confines children's learning in precisely this way, and is supported by administrators, professors, special educators and other experts who do not trust teachers to teach whole subjects to whole children.

Those who want to use the computer as an "intelligent" electronic tutor or stand-alone drillmaster are not necessarily doing something harmless. If Smith is right, much of the software on the market is either intentionally or inadvertently designed to support backward and even repressive pedagogy, which can get in the way of efforts to help students see language as a whole, become "fluent" in math, or experience the practical value and uses of communication.

You need to know what to reject, and why, as well as what to look for. Be careful not to use software that reinforces the tendency (already present in too many schools) to chop content into little unrelated parts, in an effort to spoon-feed it to students who teachers think have difficulty swallowing it whole. Rather, you should look for software expressly designed to reinforce whole language methods, to encourage question-asking as well as question-answering in math, to help your students discover the value of scientific method, to understand how a historian gathers evidence to back up conclusions, etc.

Can Drill Not Kill?

Other people claim that there is room for drill and practice. They point to programs like DLM's *Math Facts*, which works to develop speed and automaticity, or Intellimation's *Software Drill for the Mac*, which some excellent teachers have claimed to use quite creatively. Proponents of this kind of software argue that it is not the software's fault that learning is "fragmented, trivialized, and decontextualized."

Even proponents of drill and practice software usually agree, however, that such software is not the optimal use of technology in learning. Their perspective is that drill and practice software is useful IF it is used "where it belongs" in the learning process. They say that a teacher always needs first to get students receptive to what they will be taught. Next, the teacher should tell students what is going to be taught and provide them with information and mechanisms with which to manipulate the information the teacher presents. Finally, the teacher should provide the students with guided practice, with teacher support and intervention as necessary.

If all of these steps have been followed, they argue, then the "rabbit" may legitimately enter. After students have mastered the material, the teacher can turn them loose to do drill and practice on their own, in order to get better and faster. Where many teachers falter, they say, is when they jump immediately to the drill and practice, without the "teaching." *Reader Rabbit*, like all the other stand-alone software equivalents, does not teach anything. It just provides practice on material presumably mastered. Like any product, proponents of drill software argue, it does not work if it's misused.

Down with Drill

That response misses the point. The software industry is perpetuating and reinforcing an already existing and unfortunate trend in American education. When software breaks up learning into disconnected pieces, it is all that much harder for you to come up with "methods and strategies" that pull the pieces back together into a meaningful whole. If, for example, you are teaching a "whole language" approach, of what value is software that divides the whole into apparently unrelated and unconnected parts?   If your students need to get "better and faster" at a particular skill, we already have lots of materials that do not tie up the computers. As TIME Magazine has suggested, flash cards are a lot cheaper. Computers are too valuable a resource to squander. Use them for what they're good at, to promote powerful pedagogies.

Promoting Parental Involvement

- **Aren't some teachers parents?**
- **Aren't some parents teachers, too?**
- **Are parents the first teachers? the worst teachers?**

The scene: a middle school in one of the most culturally diverse neighborhoods of El Cerrito, California (and probably of the country).   A drawing is being held at a pre-Christmas parent assembly, to see which families will get to borrow the school's Macintosh computers over the Christmas vacation.   As the winners are announced, an eighth-grade girl begins jumping up and down—she cannot contain her excitement at her family's good fortune.

Scenes like the one above are all too rare in America's schools. Yet those who are interested in raising achievement levels in our nation's increasingly diverse school systems would do well to note the rich benefits such activity provides: increased parent involvement (which correlates closely with increased student achievement); creative use of computer "down time" (most of the computers in our schools are turned off for many more hours than they

are on); greater trust between school and community (a growing need especially where the student population is culturally different from the teaching
population); and increased volunteer time from parents (some of whom then
spend volunteer time within the school as well as at home with their own
children).

Parents as Resources

Teachers around the country have discovered a useful little secret: they can get
parents to help them do their job—by sending classroom computers home with
learner-centered software over weekends and vacations, by providing the growing number of families who now own computers with loaned software and at-
home learning activities, etc. Their thinking is rooted in some solid research,
which suggests that increased parental involvement in a child's schooling leads
directly to increased achievement. By learning how to help parents use the
computers sensibly at home, these classroom teachers reap the achievement
benefits of increased parental involvement with very little extra effort and very
little extra cost to the school.

These teachers are tapping into the incredible potential of at-home
computer activities as an adjunct to schoolwork. In contrast to traditional home
work assignments, these "home fun" activities can more comfortably and more

readily incorporate participation by parents and/or siblings, while still yielding big returns in student achievement. And this is only the proverbial tip of the iceberg. Imagine what teachers could do by regularly inviting parents to ally with them in doing things in the home that not only increase parental involvement, but also offer parents "quality" recreational time with their children, enhance sibling cooperation, and improve parent attitudes toward the school.

Examples of Parental Involvement

A number of school systems are already showing the way:

♦ In Charlotte, North Carolina, a fourth-grade teacher recruited a small group of parents to come to an after-school class to learn how to use computers with children, then induced them to volunteer to help her support small-group activities around her three computer stations.

♦ In Commerce City, Colorado, two paraprofessional aides (themselves parents of children in the school) organized and conducted an evening computer class for parents, as part of a weekend and vacation computer lending program. The system's computer coordinator reported some interesting results of this activity: Parents who took computers home said they were "very pleased that the school would allow this to happen." The loaning of equipment fostered a "feeling of trust and cooperation between the school and home" that had not been present before.

♦ In Arlington, Massachusetts, a group of parents volunteered to learn how to train other parents as classroom computer aides, enabling teachers to get help, for example, in supporting several cooperative groups working simultaneously on different subjects and problems at different learning stations.

♦ In Indianapolis, Indiana, fourth graders in pilot schools got "buddy" computers to keep at home during the year. Parents became more involved; students wrote work of higher quality and greater length and complexity; and students made gains in self-esteem.

Techniques to Involve Parents

All these programs rather cleverly take advantage of growing parent interest in computers, the growing willingness of parents to participate more actively in their child's learning, and the eagerness of a small but significant percentage of parents to get involved in, and give time to, their children's school. Other techniques include:

1. Giving parents who already own computers "consumer advice" about software that is fun yet still supports what the teacher is trying to do in class. A school in Massachusetts, for example, offers parents (and grandparents) reprints of software reviews just before Christmas, and guidance about where the software can be obtained at the cheapest prices.

2. Helping parents to acquire computers, either by giving them good consumer advice about how to get the best deals on the best computers, or even, in some cases, establishing systems by which parents can borrow funds to purchase computers or participate in a computer loan fund.

3. Establishing software loan programs, enabling parents to try programs before they buy them.

4. Organizing PTA or PTO sales of inexpensive learning software, as an alternative to the candy sales of the past.

5. Offering computer training to parents, for career advancement as well as student support purposes.

6. Providing circulating computer lending programs (like the one in El Cerrito) during weekends and school vacations.

Teachers are also using computers to change the way they communicate with parents. Here is how one experienced teacher described an aspect of her teaching most teachers do not even think much about:

> It was easy. I wrote a form letter and just filled in different names. I had to write the letter only once; the computer printed it out over and over. I customized each letter with specific comments about each student's performance.

One teacher has researched the effectiveness of this kind of letter writing. Parents responding to the survey were overwhelmingly in favor of the letters they received. Most parents perceived the form letters as written specifically for them. The survey results also showed that parents felt that they received more information from the teachers when the teachers used the computers than they did when more traditional methods of communication were used.

Case Study ━━━━━━━━━━━━━━━━━━ ■

Breaking Away

This case describes how Rob Johnson, a high school math teacher, overcame a variety of barriers to using computers in his classroom. The story shows how he:
- learned that computers could substantially increase student interest in math,
- discovered that computers can promote the development of higher order thinking skills, and
- discovered that computer technology readily accommodates different learning styles and abilities.

Rob remembered how reluctant he had been to change, and even begin to use technology. He laughed as he recalled how he would rant and rave in the teachers' room and at meetings about how unnecessary it was to use computers in the classroom. He had been forced to take his first step toward changing, when he used one of the *Supposer* programs to teach a lesson in his geometry class. Since his coordinator had required it, Rob insisted that she help. "If you want me to use this stuff, you'll have to help me learn how to use it." Rob decided to use the program for the one and only class that his coordinator would attend.

As he continued using the computer over the next few weeks, Rob began to notice little surprises. Text book material seemed less confusing to the students. Homework assignments seemed to improve. Most important, class interest soared. Rob decided to reexamine his feelings about computers. He decided that computers might definitely enhance the effectiveness of the curriculum he was trying to teach.

Rob's next step was to find software to use with his Algebra classes. He uncovered several programs, but ultimately chose the *Algebraic Proposer* and *Algebraic Xpressor*. He translated his normal lecture from "chalk talk" to "computer chat." He was delighted to see student interest increase. Then, as he anticipated, the kinds of questions the students asked and the nature of class discussion began to change, in a way that intrigued Rob as well as his students. He was getting more chances to talk the kind of "math talk" that he enjoyed.

A real "barrier buster" occurred one day, while teaching one of the "slower" classes, when Rob found that the visual nature of the lessons had an even more positive impact on these students than on the "top" students. Rob experienced what he came to view as his real breakthrough to integrating computers in his classroom. He had decided to allow his students to operate the computer during a lesson on linear equations. One of the students typed in a formula incorrectly, and accidentally created a hyperbola instead of a linear graph. The class quickly got caught up in this unforeseen event. "What's that thing? Did she break the computer? Why did it curve? That's neat. Let's make some more."

Rob was taken aback. What should he do? Hyperbolas were not in the curriculum for this class. Last year he would have probably told them it was created by mistake, and that they would learn about it in Algebra II. Now, with a new sense of what might be possible, he followed the cue from the students that they were ready. He taught them about hyperbolas, something he had once believed they could not learn.

After that experience, Rob began to construct a new classroom vision, one that incorporated computers as a key tool in helping to motivate students about math, helping them to visualize some of its more abstract concepts, and helping them to approach problem solving from a greater variety of directions. In his lesson plans, he began to combine the curriculum and the computer to create a more variegated approach to learning for his students. He understood that the computer could offer fresh new ways for students to learn material that was difficult for them to grasp when taught in "traditional" fashion. Whether it was his "slow" kids or his "top" kids, the computer tapped into the diverse learning styles and different kind of intelligences that his students brought to the classroom.

Now the newspaper wanted to tell his story. As he entered the office and met the reporter, he thought about the changes in his classroom. The reporter stood up, extended her hand and said, "Hi, I'm Sara. How are you, Mr. Jackson?"

"Quite different now," he said. "And so are my students. Let me tell you what's happened."

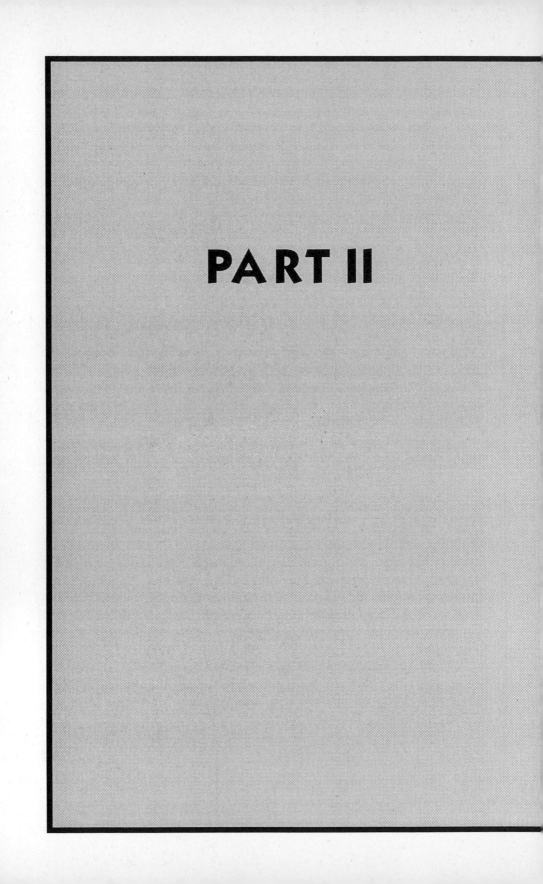

PART II

Part II of this book is comprised exclusively of practical classroom activities. Each activity is designed to enable you to put it to immediate use. We utilize five different and distinct formats in presenting these activities:

Lesson Plan

This format includes a series of categories (teacher preparation, materials needed, procedures, follow-up, and so forth) which structure the information. The Lesson Plan is the category which includes step-by-step instructions or procedures.

Unit Plan

The Unit Plan format is designed to describe a series of activities that take place over time, often a week or more. Each Unit Plan divides its materials into a small number of categories, categories which vary from unit plan to unit plan.

Up Front

In the Up Front format, the teacher doing the activity describes that activity. All the information you need to implement the activity is still included, but in a different, more personal style, with a focus on the reasons why a teacher has done certain things.

From the Sidelines

In From the Sidelines, an observer in the classroom describes what is happening. Each account concludes with a Teacher's Response, where the teacher doing the activity can respond to what the observer has written.

Kids' Perspective

The Kids' Perspective format allows students doing the activity to describe what happened, sometimes in their own words, sometimes through their work.

The classroom activities are not clustered separately into these five categories. We have purposely mixed up the activities to create some variety in what you are reading and to make it more enjoyable for you to "shop" through the various kinds of activities available.

Lesson Plan

PARALLEL LINES

Grade Level: 9-10
Time Required: 1-2 class periods

Lesson Overview
Students will explore the relationship between the linear equation and the graph of parallel lines

Where It Fits in the Curriculum
Algebra 1

Materials
3-4 computers; printer and equipment to project screen to overhead projector, *GraphWiz* and *Math Connections Algebra 1* software, teacher-prepared worksheets

Skills Students Will Develop
Recognizing patterns and predicting outcomes

Preparation
Review the software programs and make sure that some students know how to use them–at least one student for each computer.

Use the software to prepare two sets of worksheets (one on slope and one on the y- intercept). The focus of worksheets is to guide students to make connections among the coefficient of the variable, the constant in the equation, and their effect on its graph.

Grouping and Roles
Pairs of students, each student to be responsible for his or her partner's mastery of the concepts. Two to four computer groups (containing only one member of a pair) at least one student in each computer group will be Keyboarder.

Activities and Procedures
❶ Distribute a set of worksheets with problems involving linear equations to each pair. Students graph each set on the worksheet on the same set of axes, and locate intercepts.

❷ After about 15-20 minutes, designate which computers will be used for exploring Worksheet 1 and which for Worksheet 2 (1-2 each). Direct one student from each pair to a circle around a Worksheet 1 computer, the other to a Worksheet 2 group. Designate the student Keyboarders in each computer circle. Instruct them to use *GraphWiz* to graph the equations on the same set of axes. Ask students to make a quick sketch on graph paper (or make a computer printout).

❸ When the equations have been graphed along the lines, have the students rejoin as pairs to work in a Think-Pair-Share mode: Each member of the pair must explains his or her thinking about the patterns seen at the computer. They discuss what they thought about the conjectures the pair had made regarding an equation and its graph. Circulate among the pairs of students to listen to their discussions and think about which you want to have them report on in the next step of the activity.

❹ Following about ten minutes of paired discussions, select two or three students to give brief summaries of their discussions. Use the content and issues that arise in these reports to conduct a class discussion about the slope-intercept form of an equation.

Follow-Up
- Have students play *Math Connections Algebra 1: equation match* and *Math Connections Algebra 1: line match* to demonstrate and reinforce mastery.

Comments
- IBM *Math Exploration Toolkit* is also well-suited for this activity. In addition, graphing calculators would serve well.
- While I found *Algeblaster* to be too fast-paced and frustrating, students proficient with arcade games might be more ready for this challenge.

Up Front

MELTING SURFACE

I like to connect my math instruction to real-life settings, but I'm not totally confident about my scientific knowledge. So when Ed Sommes, one of the science teachers, approached me about doing something together to help the kids understand solids, I was eager to try. We wanted our students to investigate how an object's shape affects its ability to maintain heat.

The students' first activity was to find out what would be the best arrangement for 27 blocks of ice to minimize the melting. I began by saying: "Let's discover if there's anything about an object's shape that affects heat loss. We'll start with a block of ice consisting of 3 cubes frozen together (in a row). If you break it into 3 separate blocks, what do you notice?"

The students were paired up to work on the project. Ed and I handed out a spreadsheet worksheet that we had prepared ahead of time. The pairs were to use it to collect and organize data on the number of faces and the total area of the exposed faces (i.e., surface area). We also gave each pair of students several cubes to manipulate to help them determine the faces and areas. As the students organized our data, they were soon able to calculate the number of faces as well and the total surface area before and after breaking the blocks of ice.

B7		=(A7-2)*4+2*5	
		Cube SS (SS)	
	A	**B**	**C**
		# of faces before breaking	# of faces after breaking
		Assume that the area of each face = 1 sq. in.	
# of cubes in block			
	3	5 + 4 + 5 =	6 + 6 + 6 =
	4	5 + 4 + 4 + 5 =	6 + 6 + 6 + 6 =
	5	22	30
	6	26	36
	7	30	42
	8	34	48
	9	38	54
	10	42	60
	11	46	66

As the students worked, Ed and I circulated among them, answering and asking questions. About ten minutes before the end of the class, Ed conducted a discussion about the properties of melting ice. Then I guided students in discussing what we had learned about the surface area of shapes

At the end of the class, we assigned each student a row from the worksheet and told them to conduct an experiment at home, looking for any relationship between the number of faces exposed and the rate of melting, and record their data in a new column.

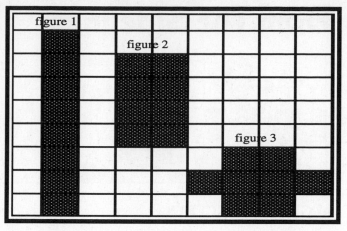

The next day, all the students reported finding that the blocks made with fewer exposed faces took longer to melt. Ed and I then had the partners return to their worksheets and cubes to look for a systematic way to arrange the blocks so as to reduce the number of faces. Using the strategy of starting with a simpler problem we used the computer-simulated tiles in *Hands-on Math* (Ventura) to quickly create activity cards with templates of possible block arrangements.

Ed and I acted as facilitators as we prompted our students with such questions as, "What happens if you stack them? Where should you divide the blocks to layer them? What is the least number of faces that can be exposed?" Some of the kids glued sugar cubes to form the blocks, not only to help with spatial perception but also to have a model for examining order and regularity. Again they found the spreadsheet a very useful tool to help them organize, calculate and analyze data on the types of cubes and the lines of symmetry we observed.

H4			=(B4*B2)+(C4*C2)+(D4*D2)+(E4*E2)+(F4*F2)+(G4* G2)						
	A	B	C	D	E	F	G	H	I
1				FACES EXPOSED					
2	figure	0	1	2	3	4	5	surface area	lines of symmetry
3	1	0	0	0	0	6	2	34	1
4	2	0	0	0	4	4	0	28	2
5	3	0	0	2	0	4	2	30	1
6									

Teacher Tips:

Once they determined the volume, they used a spreadsheet to enter volume formulas for all kinds of shapes, and solved for our respective parts to then calculate total surface area for these various shapes. Ed was pleased when someone suggested they also explore the lines of symmetry for all the shapes.

From The Sidelines

ALGEBRA CONCEPTS

Bev just finished reading *Research Within Reach: Secondary School Mathematics* published by the NCTM. She had not realized how variable and equation have different meanings depending upon context. For example, for most early adolescents the equal sign means "here comes the answer after performing some operations," rather than an indicator of equivalence. Letters can be used as a numerical value, as a shorthand for an object, as a specific but unknown number, as a generalized number, or as a range of unspecified values with a systematic relationship. She realized that providing activities that are more pictorial than symbolic and that build a bridge from arithmetic to generalized arithmetic to algebra would help her students construct several levels of meaning for variables and equations.

She read how algebra tiles (Ventura's *Algebra Concepts*) could be used to represent the generalized number notion of variables.

> Think of a number. Add 4 to it. Multiply the result by 2. Subtract 6. Divide by 2. Subtract the number you first thought of. I bet I can read your mind—your answer is 1

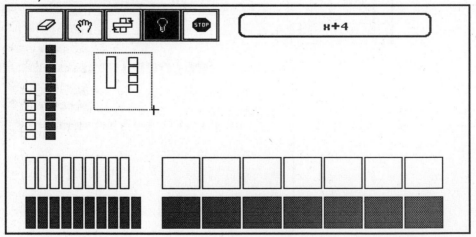

For pre-algebra students, researchers suggested that discussion of patterns or rules into symbolic or algebraic form should be preceded by exercises like the following: (She used Ventura's *Hand-On Math* color tiles to create this.)

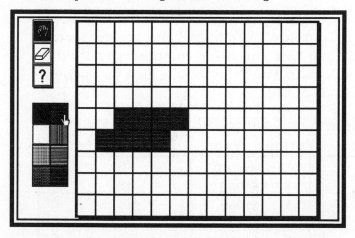

How many light tiles are needed for 10 dark tiles? 15 dark tiles? 20? 50?
Can you make a connection between the number of light and dark tiles?

She would then have students follow this by describing and representing relationships with tables, given the following:

Working with tiles, can you add tiles to this figure to make a new figure with a perimeter of 20 units? Tiles must touch each other along an entire edge (not corner to corner).

Organize your findings by how many edges the additional tiles touch. Is there a pattern between this number and the perimeter?

Once students found different ways to add tiles to get this perimeter, she asked them to find the smallest number, then the largest number of tiles that can be added. She collected and organized the class data. They discovered that a rectangle used the most tiles. What other rectangles have a perimeter of 20? And what about area? With their data, they made graphs with the length versus the width, and the length versus the area. They found out that the rectangle with the greatest area for a fixed perimeter is a square. She had laid the intuitive groundwork for the calculus concept of maximum and minimum values!

97

The Kids' Perspective

STATISTICAL HISTOGRAMS

So, O.K., I admit it. I thought that taking Sullivan's statistics course would be an easy way of satisfying my last math requirement. Hey, it's my senior year and everybody knows how to find an average; and all the newspapers and magazines use bar graphs. So it should be easy, right? Wrong! When Mr. Sullivan announced that for our first project we would have to create our own graphs and write a report, I wondered what I'd gotten myself into. Then, on top of it, Sullivan says that we have to use some computer program called *Statistics Workshop.* If I'd wanted to work with computers, I would have selected a computer class!

Well, not so "wrong" after all. Here's what happened. Sullivan divided us into groups of four (All the groups seemed pretty balanced among kids who knew computers and didn't, nerdy kids and cool kids like me, and so on.) First we opened a data file named CLASS SCORES.

					CLASS SCORES
Row	**Name**	**Period**	**Year**	**Test 1**	**Test 2**
1	Chris	First	Senior	75	81
2	Pat	First	Soph	82	84
3	Jim	First	Soph	88	86
4	Carla	First	Junior	85	88
5	Jim	First	Junior	90	89

We had to look at how the information was organized into five columns. Then we had to choose "Histogram" from the View menu. And up comes this histogram thing on screen. It was cool.

(By the way, with Paulette hitting the keys and telling us what she was doing, I right away caught on to how to use the program. Sullivan says each person in the group will get a chance to be Keyboarder, so I'm gonna be ready.)

Sullivan tells us we'll be concentrating on this histogram thing, but first he wants us to see all the other plotting features of this program. So we played with the View menu to see a bar chart, a box plot, and a scatter plot. I've got to say I felt a bit nervous about all these new types of things to learn about, but somehow the program seemed like it was going to help me a lot (and be fun to fiddle around with).

After about ten minutes, Sullivan gave each group a

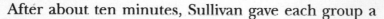

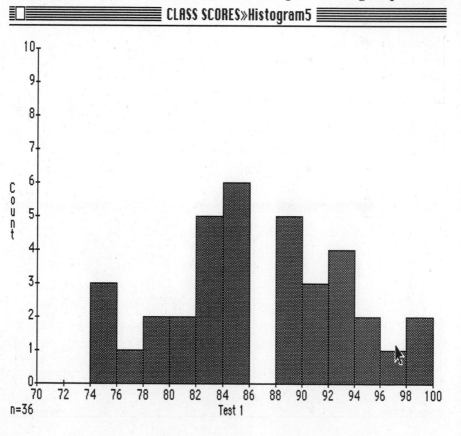

copy of the datafile and explained how the axes were set up and illustrated one way to represent the data. What a surprise when we changed the interval from 2 to 5. We printed both histograms, with the mean and median reported, so we could compare them.

Boy, did I resist the next part of the assignment: to create scenarios that explained who might prefer which histogram from four different intervals Mr. Sullivan directed us to use. But listening to the ideas of the kids in my group and giving my ideas, and talking about it all together really helped me.

It was really fun to use the "Subview" feature to compare and contrast data like the girls' with the boys', or upperclass-

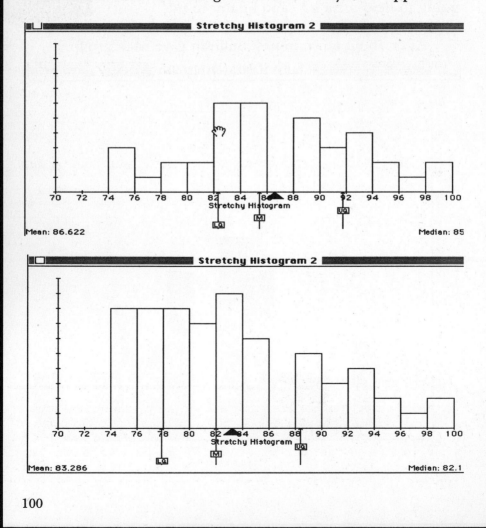

men versus underclassmen. But the "Stretchy Histogram" feature blew us away. When you choose it, a hand-cursor appears that lets you change the heights of the bars. And guess what? The mean and median change.

Mr. Sullivan had copied these screens onto overhead transparencies so he could overlay them on the overhead projector for us all to look at during the discussion we had afterwards. He also converted each graph back to a datafile and distributed a hardcopy to each group so they could discuss what happened to the data as a result of the change.

For tomorrow's class each group's challenge is to create a stretchy histogram with these three criteria:

a) The mean must be less than the median.
b) The mean must equal the median.
c) The upper quartile must equal the median.

Then we're going to create histograms that looked like these shapes. I'm really looking forward to it.

And then we have to describe any relationships we can find about the mean and median. I hate the writing part, but working as a group, we can write up our stuff pretty well.

Teacher Response:

Another neat feature of this software is that it gives the students a moveable line to explore how to fit the line to the data on a scatter plot, with a "fitmeter" (a device that measures how closely the data and the line coincide).

Lesson Plan

A PIZZA π

Grade Level: 9-11
Time Required: 1-2 class periods

Lesson Overview

Students will investigate the value of π by measuring objects and calculating the circumference/diameter ratio.

Where It Fits in the Curriculum

Geometry, measurement

Materials

- Objects such as coffee cans, saucers, soup cans, etc. that have a diameter
- Measuring stick or sewing tape (metric if you wish)
- Thread or string to measure the circumference of each object
- Computer; printer; equipment to project monitor to overhead projector
- Any spreadsheet software and *The Geometer's Sketchpad* (Key Curriculum Press)

Skills Students Will Develop

Understanding the value and meaning of π.

Preparation

Become familiar with the spreadsheet software to be used as well as *The Geometer's Sketchpad* program. Prepare the spreadsheet template for measurements and calculations, and print a copy for use in student groups. Instruct students to each bring two circular objects to class.

Grouping and Roles

Groups of three or four to share the tasks of measuring and recording. Plan for the roles of Keyboarder, Recorder, and Materials Manager. All students should take turns measuring.

Procedures and Activities

❶ Divide the students into small groups and explain to them that they will be measuring the items they have brought to class and recording their measurements. Assign roles. Distribute one spreadsheet worksheet to each group. Have them first write in the names of their group's items in the first column.

❷ With thread and measuring stick, have students take turns measuring the circumference and the diameter to the nearest tenth of a centimeter of each of their group's items. The Recorder is responsible for seeing that each measurement is correctly listed on the worksheet.

❸ Using the LCD, demonstrate how the spreadsheet program works. Have each Keyboarder enter his or her group's measurements into the computer. Show how the spreadsheet program performs all calculations.

❹ Print the resulting spreadsheet and distribute a copy to each student to take as homework along with the following questions to think about and make notes on:
- What difference does approximate vs. precise measurement make when comparing diameter to circumference?
- If you change the measurements to inches, what effect does it have when you compare diameter to circumference?

❺ Resume small grouping and have students discuss their interpretations of the spreadsheet information and the thought questions. After five to ten minutes, ask each group to agree on a conjecture about the relationship of the diameter to the circumference and to prepare a statement about how the issues of approximation, precision, and units of measurement might affect calculations.

❻ Bring the class together for discussion of these ideas. Have each Recorder present his or her group's conjecture and statement. Each group's Keyboarder then verifies their conjectures by using *Geometer's Sketchpad* to construct a circle, measure its parts, calculate the c/d ratio, and manipulate the circle to illustrate the constancy of π Students will be amazed when they see how their many variations do not affect the ratio.

Comments
- Version 2 of *The Geometer's Sketchpad* allows you (as does a spreadsheet) to create tables and add entries for measured values that change as you manipulate your figure.
- *Geometry Inventor* is also suitable for this activity.

Lesson Plan

ALGEBRA REVIEW

Grade Level: 8-9
Time Required: 1 class period

Lesson Overview

Students in teams will compete in a problem-solving competition. Teams will score points for both solving the problem AND explaining the solution.

Where It Fits in the Curriculum

Since the questions and problems can vary, the "game" model is appropriate anywhere. It is most beneficial, however, as a review technique.

Materials

Algebra textbook. A computer with LCD panel. *Algebraic Xpresser* (William K. Bradford Co.). *Algebraic Xpresser* software is a symbol manipulator and graphing software for manipulating and solving algebraic expressions.

Skills Students Will Develop

Mastery of the curriculum area being exercised, deeper understanding of the concepts through reporting solutions.

Preparation

Review use of the software, *Algebra Xpresser*. Students should know how to enter data to solve problems.

Grouping and Roles

Small groups. In each group, the *reporter* role is to articulate the group's logic and the *computer user* role is to run the software at the computer.

Procedures and Activities

❶ Divide the class into groups and designate the *computer user* and *reporter* for each group. Explain that groups will vie to solve problems that you present and the first group to explain the solution correctly and/or get the correct answer wins the points for each problem. Five points will be awarded for each of those two tasks. The group with the most points wins.

❷ Selecting problems from a text, give the first problem. The first group to correctly describe the solution gets 5 points and the opportunity to solve the problem at the computer. If they achieve the correct answer at the computer, they get 5 more points. Otherwise, another group comes to the computer to get the answer.

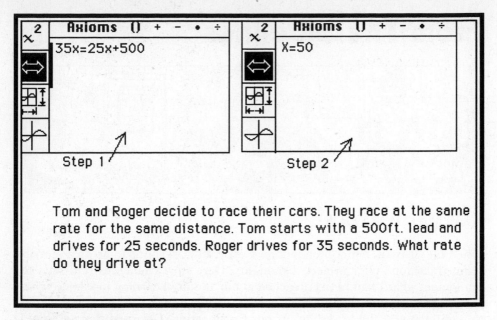

2 x.	**Axioms** () + – • ÷		2 x.	**Axioms** () + – • ÷
⇔	35x=25x+500		⇔	X=50

Step 1 ↗   Step 2 ↗

Tom and Roger decide to race their cars. They race at the same rate for the same distance. Tom starts with a 500ft. lead and drives for 25 seconds. Roger drives for 35 seconds. What rate do they drive at?

Follow-up Activities/Extensions

Students or teams can create problems for others to solve. Each team can prepare 5 or 10 problems (complete with answer and solution steps) to exchange with another team.

Comments and Hints

Having a student of average ability act as the *reporter* for each group helps increase discussion and learning within the group. The discussion required to make the *reporter* understand the solution helps everybody learn more.

From The Sidelines

NEW MATHEMATICS

When the Assistant Superintendent for Curriculum asked me to be on a "curriculum transition" pilot project, I thought, "Here's my chance to find ways to implement what I had heard preached at our Inquiry Learning in-service workshop." I would work with other teachers to create answers to the questions I'd thought about at the workshop. At our first meeting, I learned that we would develop new thinking about inquiry, cooperative learning, and technology. With little knowledge of these areas, I was optimistic that the pilot project would lead me to an entry point into all this new education. As we researched options, I concluded that it's a lot easier to say you'll change than to actually do it. Once you decide to abandon your usual approach, you are faced with unlimited options–a frightening possibility. Thank goodness I wasn't alone.

Jessica King became a sort of beacon for the rest of us. She took the plunge in her own classroom first, and I arranged to observe several of her classes. She chose *The Factory* from Wings for learning, software that simulates a "factory" that manufactures squares, with holes and stripes drawn on the surface. The holes and stripes differ in size or shape and can be placed by turning the square. The trick is to see a final product and replicate the manufacturing steps that it took to build it. Students have to design a plan to turn the shape, punch holes, and paint stripes.

Ms. King had arranged her eighth-grade class into two groups for a contest. The teams were loud, but she later told me she began to notice something. Unlike her typical classes, where she had to force many students to respond, she saw many usually quiet students beginning to take charge. *The Factory* was, however, software the kids had used in elementary school. She said she was looking for what kinds of activities might represent the appropriate next step for them.

When next I visited, she was trying out *Superfactory*. In that program, students see three sides of a cube, and have to create a plan for manufacturing the object. Ms. King had divided the class this time into several small groups of four students. She had made sure that each group had a full range of abilities. The students were working in a clearly defined cooperative structure, with each having a clear role and a well-defined responsibility to the group.

She began the session by giving each group one die, and asked them to explore the markings (dots). By connecting her Apple II computer to a large screen TV monitor, she then showed the whole class a view of one die. Each team had to plan a series of turns and moves that would make their die match the one pictured. The idea was to do so with as few moves as possible. She encouraged them to discuss their ideas, try them out with the die they had. When the group had decided upon the series of moves, they were to write them down. With this practice under their group belt, each group was ready to try manipulating a computer cube using *Superfactory.* They would manufacture a cube, in a way similar to how they had built squares with the *Factory* software.

In subsequent classes, Jessica introduced more creative challenge activities. She brought in small single-serving cereal boxes. Each group took one apart to examine how it looked as a two dimensional object. Each group had to design a copy that could be folded into a cube like the original cereal box. Then they had to create one on the computer. She encouraged her students to find and bring in other three dimensional objects for groups to try to create on the computer. The kids were hooked and so was I.

Jessica's brave start with using computers to incorporate inquiry, cooperative learning, and technology in the study of geometry gave the rest of us courage to take the plunge in other areas of the math curriculum. Based on my own observation of Jessica, I am convinced that there are at least three key elements to success in such endeavors:

- choosing software that meets kids where they are as well as meeting the needs of your curriculum,
- providing a clearly explained, explicit structure in which the students will work,
- giving kids chances to contribute to the activity with ideas, materials, and abilities of their own.

Teacher Response:

1. For me the secret of finding the right software is lots of time exploring the possibilities AND playing with it enough myself to feel confident about how it can be used. In addition to how you select and introduce the software, it is crucial that you emphasize the collaborative nature of the activity. I wanted my kids to learn from each other by teaching and sharing with each other. Somehow that multiplied the learning advantage for them.

2. Be sure to have your groups log each of their moves. Articulating what they are doing helps students clarify and reinforce what they are learning. At the same time the verbal exchanges as the team works together to get their log right enhances their enjoyment of the process.

Up Front

LONG DISTANCE RATES

When I found out I'd be teaching the ninth grade General Mathematics class, I realized that the math abilities students needed for everyday life in today's society are no longer met by a computation-based course covering the same old topics from the sixth grade. I would try to use calculators and computers to bring in problems that would move students beyond computation and capture their interest. Since I found myself using a spreadsheet both at school and at home, I thought this might be a good tool to start with. Also I knew the kids had been introduced to spreadsheets as a part of their eighth-grade computer literacy course.

The TV commercials about the pricing battles of long-distance phone companies were my inspiration for a lesson based around telephone bills. I prepared the worksheet below and distributed it, along with a calculator for every three students. I also explained how to use the worksheet's chart to find the cost for long-distance phone calls:

The cost of a long-distance telephone call changes depending on what time of day you call, where you are calling, and how long you talk.

From Boston to:	Day 8:00a.m.- 5:00p.m.		Evening 5:00p.m.-11:00p.m.		Night 11:00p.m.-8:00a.m	
	1st min.	addl. min.	1st min	addl. min.	1st min.	addl. min.
Chicago	.53	.41	.33	.23	.21	.17
Boulder	.58	.41	.39	.30	.26	.18
Dallas	.63	.47	.41	.31	.29	.20
Atlanta	.50	.40	.36	.29	.25	.20
New York	.35	.30	.25	.15	.18	.10

Use the chart above to answer these questions:

1. How much will it cost for you to call from Boston to Chicago at 9:00 p.m. and talk for 10 minutes?
2. What will the same call cost if you call at 11:05 p.m. instead?
3. Which costs more, to call New York at 7:00 p.m. for fifteen minutes, or to call Atlanta at 7:00 a.m. for ten minutes?

I instructed my students to answer the questions using the calculators, in hopes that that would help them to understand the algorithm involved to compute the cost. Next, I asked them to write in words a rule for calculating the cost of a long-distance call during the daytime. (The writing would make it easier for the students to enter the formula into the spreadsheet when we began work on the computer.)

When they finished entering the formula in columns D and E, they were astounded when I demonstrated the pull down feature from the menu, which made it so easy to complete columns D and E. After they had experimented with the cost of daytime calls by changing the values in column D on the spreadsheet, the students' next task was to complete the spreadsheet for the evening and night totals. I walked around the room and listened as students discussed how to calculate those costs, and which variables to enter into the formulas. I was pleased by the level of interaction.

I concluded by announcing that students' grades for this activity would be based on how their group solved the following problem:

> Your best friend is moving out-of-state, to California. Find out the pricing policy of MCI, Sprint, and AT&T from the promotional materials gathered on the side table, and then devise the best plan to keep in touch with your friend via telephone.

Teacher Tips:

1. Because it is so easy to make a mistake using a technology tool, I explained the importance of using estimation to check one's work on a spreadsheet. For example, the estimate for a 10-minute call to Boulder is $.60 + ($.40)*9 = $4.20, reasonably reflects the total computed on the spreadsheet.

2. I had to keep myself from helping them figure out what to do, but I did advise them to consider acceptable times to call, given time zone diferences.

109

Lesson Plan

ALGEBRAIC DIET

Grade Level: 7-8
Time Required: 1-2 class periods

Lesson Overview
Students will create and solve equations with at least one variable, using a calorie counting activity.

Where It Fits in the Curriculum
Understanding variables, equations, elementary algebra, problem solving.

Materials
A way to project the computer screen on a TV monitor or LCD panel, *Algebra Xpresser* (William K. Bradford Co.), calculators, caloric information for common foods.

Skills Students Will Develop
Setting up equations, simplifying and factoring equations, problem solving.

Preparation
The students need to have been introduced to easy algebraic equations and variables.

Grouping and Roles
No special grouping is required. Students can work in pairs or as a class.

Procedures and Activities
❶ Introduce the activity as a lunch analysis. Have students list what they had for lunch today or yesterday. List caloric information either in real numbers (e.g., two tablespoons of peanut butter = 224 calories), or adapt it to suit skill levels. For example, caloric counts for each food group could be in increments of 100 (dairy items = 200 calories per cup; grains = 300 calories per cup, etc.)

❷ Challenge the class to find a relationship among the values and create a formula for the meal.
For example: $x = 100$ calories and a meal $= ax + bx + ...nx$.

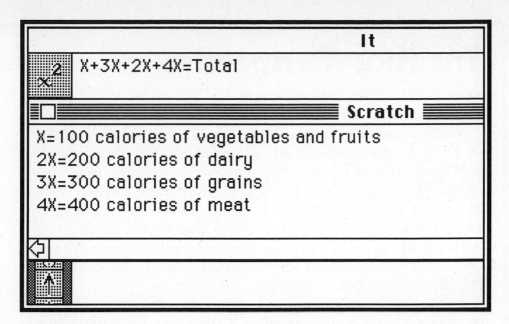

It

X+3X+2X+4X=Total

Scratch

X=100 calories of vegetables and fruits
2X=200 calories of dairy
3X=300 calories of grains
4X=400 calories of meat

❸ Use the software to present the different equations, and analyze the caloric content of the various meals. Here students can suggest factoring possibilities and simplifications, as well as plot graphs.

❹ Have pairs of students practice planning other meals and calculating the and graphing the relative caloric content of each.

Follow-up Activities/Extensions
The problems can be extended by adding additional parameters.
- Use fractions to indicate portions that are only partially eaten.
- Use different variables to represent dairy, cereals and grains, meats, and fruits and vegetables.

Comments and Hints
- Create a function called lunch that will plot calories. This could move beyond linear functions.

The Kids' Perspective

STRETCHING TO THE ANSWER

When we got to the room, an Apple IIe computer was all set up in front, with the overhead attached. Up till now, the only computers we ever used were in the lab, when we took the computer literacy course last year in fifth grade. When Mr. Richards turned on the computer, the big screen looked just like a geoboard, with dots all over the screen, and it was–in a way. He stretched a "computer simulated rubber band" from one dot to another and another until it made all kinds of shapes, like triangles, squares etc.

One of the things we liked about this program was the reporting tools it had included in it. We could ask the computer to tell us how long, or big, or whatever these shapes

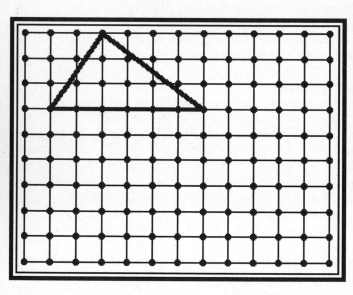

were. When we had to "solve" problems later, those tools turned out to be really necessary. In fact, they saved our necks.

We all wanted to try it immediately, but first Mr. Richards put us into five groups, each with a geoboard to practice on. Two other computers were set up in the back corners, so that when our group needed to try out our answers, we'd send one member to grab a free computer. (It was a bit messy when other groups were ready to work all at the same time, but Mr.

Richards sort of policed that scene, so that we'd all take turns.)

We had most of the period to solve a bunch of tasks. Good old Richards, those tasks were full of stuff we'd been learning about in class. Things like:

1) Create three different non-quadrilateral shapes, each with a
   perimeter of 30.
2) Design three different types of triangles, each with an area of 18.
3) Create four different shapes with a perimeter of 24.

We would have never gotten the answers without the computer. The geoboards helped, but when we needed figure-it-out time, the computer was the only help. Our group would create a guess and ask the computer to "tell" us some information. With the information we began to "correct" ourselves.

Later, each group reported its answers, using the computer in the front of the room to demonstrate. It was sort of neat how many answers kids came up with. Most every group's solutions looked a little different. Anyway, I loved using the computer and the software. (Its name is called *Elastic Lines*.) This was an awesome way to do math.

Teacher Response:

1. Elastic Lines is published by Wings for learning/Sunburst and is available on Apple and IBM platforms.

2. Software that emulates hands-on materials like geoboards actually provides a very important supplement, as well as a useful substitute, to the hands-on material itself. It often makes the difference in many students' ability to comprehend the conceptual implications of the hands-on work.

Lesson Plan

21: A LESSON IN PROBABILITY

Grade Level: 7-8
Time Required: 1 class period

Lesson Overview
Students play the card game "Twenty One," with card counting, i.e., tracking each card played using a computer. For each card dealt, they use this knowledge to "play the odds," in order to attempt to win the game.

Where It fFts in the Curriculum
Relates to curriculum goals *re* percentages, basic math operations, problem solving, and probability.

Materials
Playing Cards, calculators, and any spreadsheet software, such as *Microsoft Works, AppleWorks*, etc. Requires capacity for projecting computer screen on a larger screen, via classroom TV monitor or LCD panel.

Skills Students Will Develop
Students learn to calculate the probability of both independent and dependent events, working with fractions and percentages. Students also develop data management skills at the computer, and to analyze their own thinking strategies.

Preparation
Set up the software to tally all cards played. It should account for each card played and provide a running total of the cards played. This public information will be used by the groups to plan their strategies while playing the game.

Grouping and Roles
Cooperative groups of four or more. In each group, the *calculator* uses the calculator to calculate odds, the *spokesperson* indicates the groups decision, and at least two *advisors* analyze the computer data and recommend options to the *calculator* for ascertaining the odds for the options.

Procedures and Activities
❶ Assign students to groups and designate roles. Select a student (or two, who take turns) to account for and enter data into the spreadsheet on the computer, and two other students to act as card dealer and scorekeeper.

❷ As teams take their turn in playing Twenty One, have each card entered into the computer as it's played. All visible cards may be accounted for by number as shown here:

Ace	2
King	3
Queen	2
Jack	1
Ten	4
Nine	0
Eight	0
Seven	2
Six	1
Five	3
Four	4
Three	0
Two	4
# Played	26

❸ The data in the computer must be visible for the groups at all times. All the groups play the same hand, but may select different actions. For example one group may ask to be "hit," but another may not.

❹ After a playing session of about 15 minutes, the team with the best record of wins against the house at the end of play, is the grand winner.

❺ Conclude with a whole group discussion of strategies and observations that students used during play. Explore together notions of probability, such as the role of the 10 and the face cards, the number of cards in a deck, the number of suits, etc.

Follow up Activities/Extensions
- Assign a group to play the game without access to the data base. Track their results as compared to groups who have access to the data. Note the variance and discuss possible reasons.
- Play the games with time limits.

Comments and Hints
Take time outs frequently during the game for analysis of strategies. Use this opportunity to double check the math thinking of the students.

Up Front

ALGEBRAIC GRAPHS

I still enjoy teaching, after sixteen years. But I need to find fresh ideas to keep it that way. With my ninth-grade advanced-placement class, I'd already used the computer quite a bit. Every Friday, the students used a game called the *Factory* by Wings for learning. The software is set up to produce a particular object through a series of operations similar to activities on an assembly line: punching holes, turning the work, painting stripes, thus simulating a "factory" that manufactures squares, with holes and stripes drawn on the surface. The holes and stripes differ in size or shape and can be placed by turning the square. The trick is to see a final product and replicate the manufacturing steps that it took to build it. One activity is to reproduce each object the computer selects as a challenge. My students used it as a game competing to see who could make the most correct copies with the fewest moves. They asked to play it again and again, and I enjoyed their excitement. But I felt it was time to see how I could use the computer with the "basics" of the math class. I searched for something to fit my current curriculum–algebraic functions–and came up with another Wings for learning program, called *Green Globs.*

Upon examining the software, I was really pleased with some of the possibilities. *Green Globs* is a game that places thirteen randomly scattered globs on a grid. Players are challenged to enter algebraic equations to plot lines that explode globs as the graph line passes through the globs. The scoring algorithm gave more points for equations that pass through a number of globs at a time. Players have to apply what they know about various types of equations (e.g. linear, quadratic, inverse etc.) to win.

When Friday came around, I introduced the new game. To my surprise, the students were really tentative at arriving at solutions. They did well at plotting linear equations but were confused by the other equations. I was puzzled because these kids do so well on the exams. Over the weekend, I thought about it and realized that this was a real opportunity. The NCTM standards and educational reform efforts began to make more sense now. I had encountered an instance of students having to *apply knowledge* to solve a problem.

So I revised my strategy. I would do more with graphing functions. Although my students, given a equation, could plot Cartesian coordinates, they might not be able to visualize the shape of the graph given various types of equations. I decided to "teach" the equation shape. Using an old version of graph plotting software for the Apple IIe called *Graphing Equations* by Conduit Software, I proceeded to demonstrate graphic changes caused by equation changes.

Equations	
1 Linear	$f(x) = ax + b$
2 Quadratic	$f(x) = ax^2 + bx + c$
3 Cubic	$f(x) = ax^3 + bx^2 + cx + d$
4 Quartic	$f(x) = ax^4 + bx^3 + cx^2 + dx + e$
5 Exponential	$f(x) = ab^x$

First, the class experienced linear equations, discovering the effect on the graph as the values of *a* and *b* varied. Next, they explored quadratic equations, noting the changes. I had them follow the same procedure for each of the other three other types of functions–cubic, quartic, and exponential. I also asked the students to log their results.

Now they were ready for a fresh attack on those green globs. In addition to the instructions, I made the following revisions to the class organization:

- I assigned students to teams of three;
- I gave each team a graphing calculator and graph paper;
- I assigned the job of either *calculator*, *recorder*, or *leader*.
  (Recorders were to log each equation, and the resulting graph drawn.)

With each team going in rotation, students came to the computer to study and "calculate" the functions. I moved about the classroom observing as groups planned their functions. As team members suggested solutions, others asked them to explain the reasoning behind it. What a treat to watch students trace on the screen how their function would hit the globs. They were teaching each other stuff that I never thought I could teach them. I found that particularly rewarding to see.

Teacher Tips:

1. Work your way from the simple to the complex. Kids need time to adapt to classroom changes too.

2. It's O.K. to start with the computer off to the side, but eventually the tool is most effective when it's in the center of the classroom curriculum.

From The Sidelines

THE PRICE WAS RIGHT

Sharing the teachers' room with John Eagan means enduring his constant complaints. But this time turned out different. "Review, review, review!" John groaned. "I'm so tired of review! These seventh graders never seem to learn the basics of fractions, no matter how often we do them. So how are we supposed to teach for deeper understanding?" Alas, poor John. Not only did he have to handle fraction review in his curriculum, but Betty Cooper, his department coordinator, insisted on strict compliance with the written curriculum, and John was scheduled to be observed soon. How could he address the review and "teach" more significant material?

"Why not use a computer?" someone tired of his moaning muttered. Betty had offered computers, but she could put only one or two in a classroom. John hadn't seen much use for that, but that was then. I saw him pause, the idea entering his mind. Maybe a computer — even just one or two — could help him teach more effectively. Might his kids learn concepts faster and better with computers? John really didn't know whether computers would be better, he just hoped. The idea was sown, and I watched it sprout and flourish.

Showing optimism for the first time I can remember, John began planning his review with computers. Was that actually a smile I caught crossing his face as he was outlining his emerging ideas to me over lunch? The kids would play a game he called "The Price Is Right." Using a computer spreadsheet that he would fill with price data from the grocery store, the class would be given the challenge of picking correct fractions that would meet numbers which he would give them. For example if hot dogs were $2.10 and the target goal is 98¢, then students would have to figure a fraction that when multiplied times $2.10 would equal or be close to 98¢. (Close would count. Sometimes fractions aren't exact, he explained.) The winners would receive points for the closest answers. John planned to use a *Microsoft Works* spreadsheet program with the class. He reasoned that by using a single Macintosh computer with an LCD panel for projection, he could have student teams take turns using the computer during the game. Ultimately, he chose to have a designated computer operator from each team come up.

118

Several days later, when John was ready, I dropped by his class when he was introducing the game to his students. Betty had helped him make the spreadsheet template. It was really simple. He had an *item name* column, a column for the *price*, a column to enter a *fraction* proposed, and a column to show the answer. The program would compute the arithmetic in the last column. He wanted the kids to think the math not do the arithmetic. His prices came straight from the supermarket newspaper inserts. All prices were under ten dollars. He entered a single price for each item that, when multiplied by a fraction, would equal $1.14. The class was divided into nine teams of three players; each team had a calculator. Students were assigned specific roles to play within each group.

John's computer-assisted Basics Review activity took off! Soon the kids were looking forward to it each week. As the students became more familiar with the game, Mr. Eagan began to use multi-step problems. For example, what two different prices and fractions that when summed would equal the target number? He began changing the prices with students. He used the prices for houses, cars, clothes, and other items. He encouraged teams to create challenges for each other to solve. As the idea progressed, a few students began using imperfect fractions like 5/4 to add a whole new twist to the game.

Teacher Response:

1. Do NOT stop with the first correct answer. Getting student groups to find other fractions that fit gave my students excellent opportunities to discover more about reducing fractions and common denominators.

2. Make your students' work public. As trust develops, have students discuss the "plan" or logic that got them to the answers. These "debriefings" often provided the most learning of all.

3. The grouping of students is best carried out with assigned jobs. With about three students per group, I assigned three roles: a calculator, a reporter (the one to give the group's official answer), and a computer operator. (Each group sent a representative to the computer.)

Unit Plan
TO FLY A KITE

Unit Overview
In cooperative work groups, students will design a kite. As a prerequisite for designing a successful kite, they investigate quadrilaterals and, in particular, "discover" how to find the midpoint of a quadrilateral.

Grade Level: 7-9
Time: 4-5 class sessions

Materials
Three computers, calculators, *Geometric Supposer* (Wings for learning), various materials required for kite building (newspaper, wooden or light metal rods, string, rag strips, and glue).

Instructional Preparation
Introduce the software. Several students will need be able to use the program with ease. The *Geometric Supposer's* Quadrilaterals is designed as an exploration and learning tool. Once a given shape is created on screen, one can use tools to measure it. The data created by these measurements appear in an area on the left hand side of the screen for continuing reference. Divide the class into small groups. Create groups of balanced abilities. Assign each student a role: *software expert, Chair, secretary, design engineer(s)*.

Process
For each class session, begin with a review of the task and use of the software. Provide any new instructions (see Activities below). End each class with a 5-10 minute debriefing about that session's activity. During the class period, the teacher should move among groups, facilitating student exploration, use of the software, and problem solving.

Given that the task will be to make kites that fly, the entire class first generates together a list things they will need to learn to do. In their work groups, one of the first steps must be to learn about quadrilaterals. To develop an understanding of quadrilaterals, the groups should use the software to explore questions like the following:

- What shape is created if one connects the midpoints of the sides of a given quadrilateral? (for basic understanding)
- How does one find the area of a Quadrilateral? (for calculating the surface of the kite)
- Are there any relationships between perimeter and area? (for basic understanding)

- Is there a rule for finding the midpoint of all types of quadrilaterals or does each kind have separate rules? (to recognize that kites should be connected at the midpoint)
- What are the relationships of diagonals and the

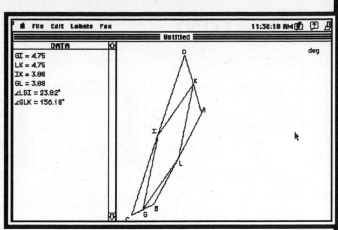

resultant quadrilateral? (for designing the frame of the kite)

Activities
Each of the following activities can take approximately one class session, including the introductory review and concluding debriefing discussion.

Have each group use the software to draw a trapezoid. Plot each side's midpoint, create another quadrilateral inside it, and then investigate the resulting quadrilateral. Have students record all data. They should continue experimenting with other trapezoids, then follow up their investigations by generating hypotheses and testing each with a variety of quadrilaterals to find one that fits all.

Given a random quadrilateral, students investigate the surface area. Their task is to find a way of predicting or calculating the area. They should try out each idea on a variety of quadrilaterals. Does the idea work with all instances of quadrilaterals?

Given a random quadrilateral, how can they calculate the exact midpoint of shape? They should test their hypotheses until they find a consistently successful way to find the midpoint of any quadrilateral.

Finally, each group should design its kite from materials available, applying the mathematical learning that they have accumulated.

Wrap-up
On a kite flying field trip, students observe the behavior of their kites and make generalizations from the results about the various designs. Members of each group then collaborate on a written (and illustrated) report of their experience from inception to flight (or flight failure).

Up Front

PROVE IT
GEOMETRY

Although last year was my tenth year teaching, in many ways it felt like my first. I took the risk to become better and surprised myself with just how far I came. I've been a good teacher, but until last year I was teaching a conventional curriculum in a conventional way. My turning point came when I read a book about using computers in the classroom. At first, my reaction was skeptical. Reading about inquiry learning and computers had me asking myself, "Is this live or is it Memorex?" The challenge of teaching the basics is hard enough. Introducing an inquiry learning approach as well reminded me of past failed educational ideas. Was I on the verge of rerunning an old reform movement? What wonderful surprises were in store for me when I discovered how to teach both inquiry and basics, while using classroom computers to boot.

On the recommendation of colleagues, I tried out the software *Geometric Presupposer* (Wings for learning). I used it to create all types of geometric shapes. With the built-in tools, I explored getting information about the shape (like the length of sides or the size of angles) and many other attributes that are vital in inquiry learning. Feeling comfortable with it, I began planning for introducing it to my class. To use the computer effectively, I decided to divide the class into small teams of three students.

I saw possibilities for an intriguing game. The object of my game would be to "prove" the nature of various shapes that I would deal out to my student teams. For instance, if I drew a circle, students in their teams would figure out together how they could prove what kind of a shape I'd made. They might read the diameter in several different directions to see whether they were all the same. If so, they'd prove that the circle was in fact a circle. Another strategy a team might decide on could be to get the circumference and compare it to see if the calculated circumference is the same as the actual. The teams would have many options and would use the computer to discover facts they could use to support hypotheses.

To maximize cooperative learning, I assigned members of each team one of three jobs: librarian, designer, or reporter. The librarian's role was to research questions using the textbook, the designer's job was to sketch solutions using graph paper, and the reporter had to announce and explain the group's process and results. Over the two periods I planned for the activity, I would rotate the roles so that each student took each role.

On the day we started the activity, I arranged the class seating according to teams. Then I demonstrated to the whole class an example of the game with a square. From the computer, I projected a square with the LCD panel. I had each team, in turn, request a single piece of information–like the length of a side or the size of an angle. When any team felt it had accumulated sufficient information to "prove" the particular shape, its reporter could ask to state the rule or attribute and proof procedure for the team. If the team was correct it got the points. The students quickly caught on. The challenge seemed quite easy. They were ready for triangles. But before letting them go on, I conducted a discussion to assess their grasp of the concepts and to encourage them to describe the process they were using to solve the problems.

Next, I projected right triangles. As we changed to acute, obtuse, equilateral, and isosceles triangles, the questioning period lengthened. At first, only a few teams used their librarian for research, but as the game progressed, more librarians were looking up information. Along with their graph paper, the kids used calculators often as they gathered facts to prove their cases. By the end of class, I was pleased to see the changes in the group's inquiry process. I asked them to write about their experience as homework follow up and preparation for playing again.

We used the whole class period this first time. The next time, I rotated team roles for half the period, held a debriefing discussion, and then rotated for the second half. I also chose students to run the software, selecting the shapes to project. Later in the year, as students were exposed to other shapes, we resumed the game.

Teacher Tips:

1. How many points teams earn per problem is not important. Keep it simple and out of the way of the real business of inquiry. One point per problem solved was fine with my class; yours might enjoy seeing a 100-point gain each time they succeed.

2. In assigning students to teams, mix different styles of learning and methods of working. Give team members interdependent jobs.

3. Software programs like the Supposer series are tremendous as inquiry tools. Students need time and encouragement to learn to interrogate objects with the software. In general, previous schooling has trained them to find the "one right answer," or the one best way (= the teacher's way?). Inquiry learning supports finding any one of several paths to the "answer." It empowers student learning and builds enthusiasm for mathematics.

Lesson Plan

DECODE OR NOT DE CODE?

Grade Level: 11-12
Time Required: 1-2 class periods

Lesson Overview
Students will learn about use of numbers for coding, and explore various matrices for coding.

Where It Fits in the Curriculum
Discrete mathematics, application of matrices

Materials
Computer; printer; equipment to project screen to overhead projector; *MathCAD* software; decoding worksheet

Skills Students Will Develop
Applying properties of matrices and matrix multiplication

Preparation
Make student worksheets by using any word processing program to turn a passage of text into simple substitution code by assigning a number to each letter of the alphabet and then using Replace to change the passage into all numbers. Some students as well as yourself should be familiar with how to use the software.

Grouping and Roles
Whole class, the role of inputter (to enter information for the *MathCAD* program) can be rotated among class members.

Procedures and Activities
❶ At the close of class one day, discuss with students the concept of secret codes based upon simple substitution, where each letter always translates into the same code. Point out that since E and T are the most common letters of the English alphabet, code-breakers can quickly determine the codes for E and T and then go on to deduce the rest of the message from other common words. Using T and E, for instance, what would be the most likely next letter the code breakers would identify? How would they then be able to try code for Y and N? Distribute copies of your coded passage for students to try to decode before the next class.

124

❷ With student interest in numeric coding piqued, introduce the concept of Matrix Coding as follows: In 1929-31, a mathematician named Lester Hill created a way to use matrices to encode messages that made the coding more complicated. Here's how he did it.

❸ Using the chalk board, overhead projector, or a poster with the steps on it, go over each step in Hill's Matrix Coding procedure.

He first assigned every letter to an integer using an arithmetic sequence:

Matrix Code

A:	...,	-51,	-25,	1,	27,	...,	$26n + 1$, ...
B:	...,	-50,	-24,	2,	28,	...,	$26n + 2$, ...
C:	...,	-49,	-23,	3,	29,	...,	$26n + 3$, ...
D:	...,	-48,	-22,	4,	30,	...,	$26n + 4$, ...
E:	...,	-47,	-21,	5,	31,	...,	$26n + 5$, ...
F:	...,	-46,	-20,	6,	32,	...,	$26n + 6$, ...
G:	...,	-45,	-19,	7,	33,	...,	$26n + 7$, ...
H:	...,	-44,	-18,	8,	34,	...,	$26n + 8$, ...
I:	...,	-43,	-17,	9,	35,	...,	$26n + 9$, ...
J:	...,	-42,	-16,	10,	36,	...,	$26n + 10$, ...
K:	...,	-41,	-15,	11,	37,	...,	$26n + 11$, ...
J:	...,	-40,	-14,	12,	38,	...,	$26n + 12$, ...

Step 1
Put the letters into a square matrix: 3 x 3, for example. (Calculations with matrices of higher dimensions can be easily done by programs such as *MathCAD*.)

Example:

seventeen
$$\begin{bmatrix} s & e & v \\ e & n & t \\ e & e & n \end{bmatrix} \quad \begin{bmatrix} 19 & 5 & 22 \\ 31 & 14 & 46 \\ 57 & 83 & 40 \end{bmatrix}$$

Step 2
Multiply each square matrix by a coding or key matrix, such as

$$\begin{bmatrix} 0 & 1 & 2 \\ 1 & 2 & 3 \\ 2 & 3 & 4 \end{bmatrix}$$

(Use *MathCAD* to perform the matrix multiplication.)

Step 3

Change the resulting matrix back to letters to write the coded message.

Step 4

Repeat these steps as often as needed, within the largest square matrix the program allows, to encode a longer message.

❹ Give the students an encoded message and ask them to figure out the steps to decode the message (which are:

Step 1

Break the message up into groups of nine letters and write as matrices in the form:

$$\begin{bmatrix} 1 & 2 & 3 \\ 4 & 5 & 6 \\ 7 & 8 & 9 \end{bmatrix}$$

Step 2

Use *MathCad* to find the inverse of the key matrix and multiply each matrix by the inverse.

❺ Have students make up messages of their own and a coding matrix.

Follow-Up Activity
- Have students create their own matrix code by changing the arithmetic sequence or trying other kinds of sequences.
- Invite students to research how the business sector or the military use code.

Lesson Plan

THE VIEW THAT COUNTS

Grade Level: 10-12
Time Required: 1-2 class periods

Lesson Overview

Students will represent situations that involve variables with an equation, then investigate critical portions of a graph and interpret the graph.

Where It Fits in the Curriculum

Algebra, graphing equations

Materials

Computer, printer, and equipment to project to an overhead screen; Teacher-developed worksheets; *Math Connections: Algebra 1* (Wings for learning/Sunburst),

Skills Students Will Develop

Problem solving, mathematical connections

Preparation

Using the tools of *Math Connections*, prepare the text of the problem, its equation, table and graph. Generate worksheets for students from your file. Students will need to have familiarity with coordinate axes, functions, and graphs of functions.

Grouping and Roles

Whole class, then groups of 5-6 for discussion

Activities and Procedures

❶ Using the LCD, demonstrate how to use *Math Connections*, to create a network among the text, equation, table, and graph. Show how and where the program automatically updates all parts of the network if a change is made in any one part. (*Math Connections* is an Algebra 1 software program that lets you create a network among the text, equation, table, and graph–all in the same active window.)

A rectangular swimming pool with dimensions 30 feet by 50 feet is surrounded by a walk of uniform width x. Find the approximate width of the sidewalk if its area is 600 square feet.

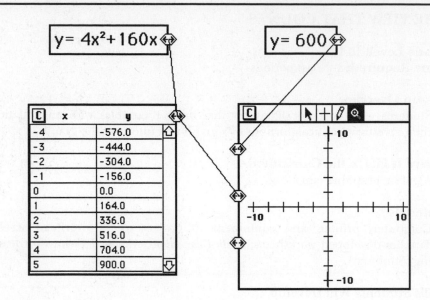

❷ Hide everything except the text and present the problem to the class. Instruct them to draw a diagram, and write an equation to solve the problem.

❸ Once everyone understands the diagram and its equation, show the table and the graph. To help make sure that students will develop a strong intuitive understanding of domain and range, have them discuss in groups what's wrong or incomplete in the picture and how to rectify it.

❹ When the groups are ready to reunite as a class, lead a discussion about the standard viewing rectangle of graphing utilities and how sometimes it is necessary to display a graph from several different viewing rectangles to describe a complete graph and all of its important features.

❺ Return to the problem. Since we are interested only in the values of x that could be possible widths of the sidewalk, then what must x be? Referring to the table, click on the border of the graph to change the maximum and minimum values for x and y.

⑥ Because we want the area of the sidewalk to be 600, the intersection of a horizontal line y =600 with the graph can be useful in zooming in to an approximate value. Use the crosshair cursor to read coordinates. Reenter values in the table to get closer values.

A rectangular swimming pool with dimensions 30 feet by 50 feet is surrounded by a walk of uniform width x. Find the approximate width of the sidewalk if its area is 600 square feet.

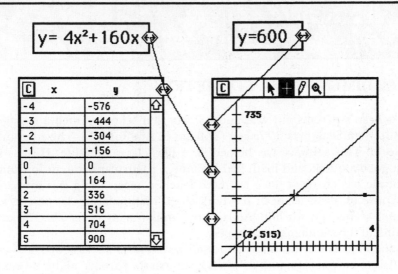

Follow-up
- Use a spreadsheet program to calculate an exact value.
- Have students solve the quadratic equation by an algebraic method.

From The Sidelines

THREE DIMENSIONAL GEOMETRY

As Sean's parents, my wife and I worry that school is such a struggle for him. But when Sean uses *3D Images* (William K. Bradford Co.), he steps into his own world. This software has helped save his "classroom" life. He has never been a good student, and math had become a particular torment for him. But his attitude has changed since his math teacher began using this software. To the surprise of all of us, Sean has flourished. Manipulating 3D objects with a computer seems easy for him. Apparently, unlike many other kids, he can see and think in three dimensional shapes.

When Ms. Heller introduced the software several weeks ago, Sean was one of the first to have success with it. When I came in for parents' night, he was a featured attraction showing the kinds of ways it can be used in math learning. He used it to create shapes like faces or goblets using basic geometric shapes in three dimension. The software has three perspectives of viewing, an X,Y, and Z axis.

By drawing and varying the viewpoint, Sean had mastered the properties of geometric shapes in a fashion different from most. Sean told us some of the ways Ms. Heller uses the program in his class. For instance, in one lesson, she began by demonstrating the basic drawing tools in the software. She then emphasized the polygon and rectangle tools and the face and extrude tools. (See manual, page 6). Then she:

- Drew a polygon in the three dimensional mode (with the extrude tool) and then showed the class how to move the shape with the axes tools.
- Directed the class to divide into work groups and go to the computer and build a design with three shapes. One time, she used three different shapes, another time, one shape in three different sizes. She then printed out the original design and rotated the shapes into a new configuration, which she saved on the disk. (These transformed designs were used in the next class as challenges for other groups to return to the initial shapes.)

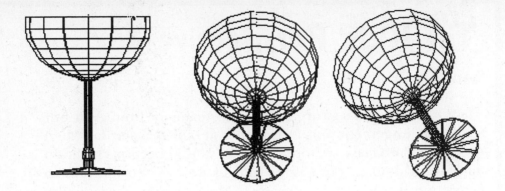

- Had each group assign a challenge to another group to see if they could use the axes tools to return the transformed designs to the original shape

Teacher Response: _____

Everyone has multiple intelligences and kids like Sean can have particularly strong visual and kinesthetic ways of approaching things. So for them the challenges of this software seem pretty easy. Other kids noticed Sean's skills using the software, and now they ask his advice when they use it. For kids like Sean, who have never been looked to for advice or help with anything in the curriculum, this development marks a kind of turning point in their academic career. AND the rest of the kids benefit too.

The Kids' Perspective

LAWS OF CHANCE

Our math class is organized into teams of four. And our seating arrangement puts us together at tables. Yesterday when we got to math class, we found a list of weird questions taped to each team's table. Mr. Cismic told us we had ten minutes to figure out the answer to as many of the questions as we could. They were doozies: In a baseball season, what could the longest winning streak of the worst team be? What would the top team record be? If we flipped a coin one thousand times, how many heads and tails would we get? How many times during the flip-

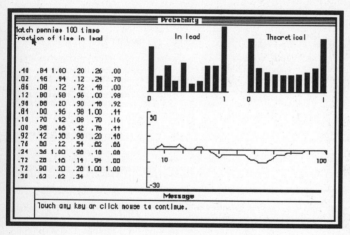

ping would the count be even? How often would we have to roll dice before the results would create a bell shaped curve? If someone took a random walk of a thousand steps, where would he end up? ...and lots more. Next to the list, Cismic had put some stuff we could use—dice, a coin, and xeroxed pages from some almanac or something.

Joe and Inez began working on the baseball questions, and Jaime and I flipped coins, counting heads and tails. Max tossed dice. We think we're a pretty good team, but when the ten minutes were up, we didn't really have much to report. The other teams hadn't done any better. So then Mr. Cismic showed us about this computer program called *Probability The-*

ory (True Basic). Using a machine that projected the computer screen on a bigger screen, the whole class worked together to reenact thousands of coin tosses and hundreds of baseball seasons in a matter of a few seconds. Having explored doing it by hand and head the hard way first, we were really aware of what we needed to do for the reenactments.

During the "random walk", for example, a dot moves along the screen, showing the steps. The program also enabled us to see graphs of our results. We discussed the results and looked for the "laws" of chance that were operating during these experiments. Having the computer flip the coin, throw the dice, etc. made one thousand a more manageable number of trials than we could ever do in real life. In our teams, we barely got started, but the computer executed thousands of trials in seconds. That made it more fun to create theories and then test them. We also talked about being able to get results both numerically and in graphs. Max and Inez are terrific with numbers, and Joe and I decided we understood results better from graphs. Of course, some brains, like Jaime, did best, because he was super quick at interpreting both the numbers and the graphs.

```
                          Probability
 7   11   .140      Theoretical              n = 10000
 8   15   .150
 9   8    .080
10   8    .080
11   7    .070
12   2    .020

 2   30   .030
 3   61   .061      2          12      2           12
 4   76   .076
 5   124  .124
 6   117  .117         n = 100             n = 1000
 7   113  .173
 8   123  .123
 9   113  .113
10   86   .086
11   73   .073
12   24   .024      2          12      2           12

                           Message
      Touch Return or click mouse to continue, Clear to quit.
```

133

Lesson Plan

MATH DATA

Grade Level: 7-9
Time Required: 1-2 class periods

Lesson oOerview

The class creates quick research studies using different types of data: continuous, discrete, Boolean, ordinal, and nominal. Students generate an example of each type of data, collect the data in a spreadsheet or database of their design, and analyze the results with appropriate statistical tools or graphs.

Where It Fits in the Curriculum

Statistics, number theory, probability.

Materials

Spreadsheet and database software. (An integrated piece of software like *Microsoft Works* or *AppleWorks* is preferable, but separate programs will also work.)

Skills Students Will Develop

Recognition of differences among these various types of data, and how the data type controls the selection of mathematical operations that are available for analysis. Students will also gain skill at making judgments from data.

Preparation

Review with the class each of the data types: continuous, discrete, Boolean, ordinal, and nominal. Also review the process of creating a spreadsheet and database in the selected software. Students will need to be aware of the data manipulation tools available for each.

Grouping and Roles

Whole class. Five recorders will write ideas and plans on the blackboard; five or more keyboarders will enter data.

Procedures and Activities

❶ Teach the five data types to the class. Select five students as recorders. Use whole class discussion to generate several information areas that match each of the types of data, which the recorders will write where all can see. For example, height (continuous), sex (Boolean), eye color (nominal), shoe size (discrete), effort grade on report card (ordinal).

❷ Have the class select one example of each data type for which they will create a mini-research plan. For each plan, have the class decide upon the data gathering instrument, the computer storage template, and the data analysis tools they will use. Have the recorders write these as they are planned.

❸ By having all students supply information in each of the five areas, gather, measure, and record the data. Use students with computer skill as keyboarders at the computer. Collect the information one area at a time. Each type of research will require a separate computer storage and analysis tool.

❹ After all the data has been recorded, invite the students to make predictions about the data. For example, if height were the continuous data selected, what would a graph look like?

❺ Follow student suggestions to explore the computer graphing tools to report the data in various formats.

❻ Discuss the results, paying particular attention to how the type of data influences the ways of reporting results.

Follow-up Activities/Extensions

Students could be asked to pose hypotheses about relationships that may appear. New research topics may flow from this activity.

Comments and Hints

This is a good introduction to real research. This activity should not be used the first time students use spreadsheets or databases.

From The Sidelines

NETWORK CONSULTANTS, INC.

As the school system's math coordinator, I had been on an unofficial tour of duty recently, loosely gathering data about how teachers were grappling with the new NCTM standards. In spite of the standards' assumptions about the important role of computers/calculators, translating them into practice in a high school math classroom was not so easy. The advantages of graphing utilities like the IBM *Math Exploration Toolkit, MathCAD*, etc., were pretty obvious. But what about tools like spreadsheets, database managers, or even word processors? It's one thing to advocate reading, writing, and critical-thinking across the curriculum; it's another thing to translate it into practice. That's why I was looking forward to my visit to Tim O'Shea's tenth grade geometry class. I had been invited to see how software was changing the study of geometry, both in content and style.

O'Shea had told me how transformations, which traditionally had been the last (and optional chapter) in most textbooks, now played a key role in helping students to deduce properties of figures and to identify congruent and similar figures. This was due, in large part he felt, to software programs like *The Geometer's Sketchpad* and the *GeoExplorer*.

Few in the class noticed me enter. In working groups at various stations around the room, students were using geoboards to explore the ideas of translation, rotation, and reflection.

REFLECTIONS

1. a) Label the coordinates of the vertices of the figure.
   b) Sketch the reflection of the figure over the y-axis. Use your geoboard to check your reflected image.
   c) Label the coordinates of the vertices of the image.
2. a) What appears to be the relationship between the coordinates of the original figure and its image?
   b) Compare your findings with others in the group. State your idea algebraically or graphically.

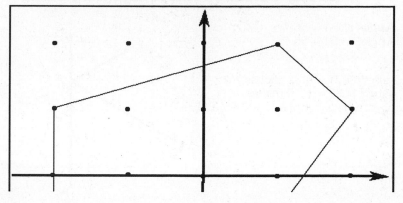

This idea can be connected to algebra by placing the figure on a coordinate plane as the *GeoExplorer* allows. Another group was using MIRAs to identify types of symmetry in the given designs and friezes.

There were groups of three at each of the three computers in the center of the room. One group was working with *The Geometer's Sketchpad's* introductory investigation into transformations. Another group was investigating properties of reflection. I was impressed at the ease in which the kids used the program, just by constructing and dragging points. Yet the power it released in understanding through visualizing was a joy to watch.

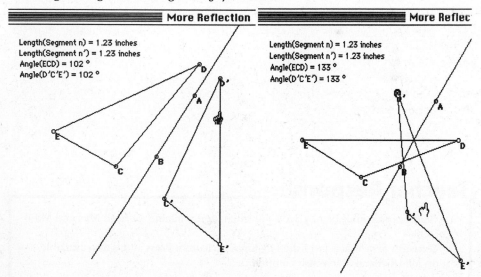

The Poolroom Math Investigation was really fun.

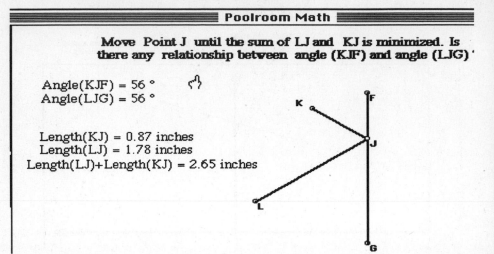

Poolroom Math

Move Point J until the sum of LJ and KJ is minimized. Is there any relationship between angle (KJF) and angle (LJG)

Angle(KJF) = 56 °

Angle(LJG) = 56 °

Length(KJ) = 0.87 inches
Length(LJ) = 1.78 inches
Length(LJ)+Length(KJ) = 2.65 inches

At each of the stations kids were actively involved and talking math to each other!

Afterwards Mr. O'Shea showed me a fantastic educational game, MECC's *The Geometric Golfer* that he was anxious to let the kids use in order to further develop their transformational skills. The object of the game is to place a ball in a hole using as few strokes as possible, as in the real game of golf. But the ball and the hole are polygons and moving the ball must be done by translations, reflections, rotations, and dilations. I was getting hooked!

Teacher Response:

1. *GeoExplorer* is published by Scott Foresman and available for both Mac and MS-DOS.
2. *Geometer's Sketchpad* is published by Key Curriculum Press and is also available on MS-DOS and Macintosh computers.

From The Sidelines

SKETCHING GEOMETRY

As the system's math/computer specialist, Beth had learned to become proficient with a variety of software programs that the schools had acquired over the years. So Beth found herself preparing more and more demonstration lessons that could be adapted to the best features of a software piece. She was currently working on a lesson for teacher training on the area of triangles. She decided she would begin with some hands-on geoboard activities that would lead into the following discussion:

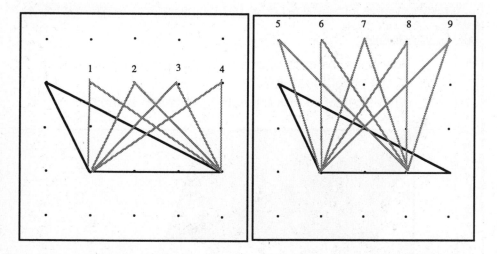

A GEOMETRIC APPROACH	AN ALGEBRAIC APPROACH
As long as the base and the height are held constant, the area will remain the same.	As long as the product of the base and the height is constant, the area will remain the same. Therefore the commutative property , 2x3 = 3x2 , allows for these possibilities.

What computer-based activities should follow that would build upon and enhance this opening activity?

She first went to the *Geometer's Sketchpad*, a drawing tool she preferred because she witnessed repeatedly how the program enables students, many of whom were awkward with compass and protractor, to construct and manipulate geometric figures so that they can actively explore and analyze important relationships/principles. But what really makes *Sketchpad* so outstanding are its scripting (record and playback constructions step-by step) and animation features. She opened the investigation on triangle area. Using the Measure menu, she found the area of the gray triangle and the area of the parallelogram. She also used the calculate option to find the area of the parallelogram by the formula. By dragging the designated point along the horizontal line, one can see the figure change dynamically. As you drag the point, all measurements and calculations automatically update. Yet the base, height, and area remained constant! (She could recall trying to demonstrate the relationship between the area of a rectangle and the area of a parallelogram in the old days with a construction paper model, folding in a triangle on one end and folding out a congruent triangle on the other end. We've come a long way!) But what she had done once or twice could now be dynamically and endlessly illustrated by *Sketchpad*. Therein lies its power: providing as many examples, variations, and data as the student needs to help him through visualizing and analyzing toward abstract generalizations.

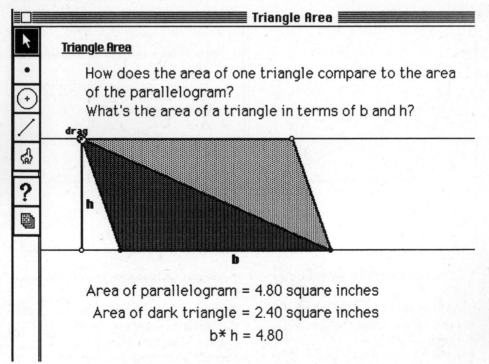

She then went to the *Geometric Supposer,* one of the first generation drawing tools. While it was not possible to illustrate these same ideas with the *Supposer* Triangle program, she did find that it could be used to show that the area could be calculated using any of its altitudes and respective bases. Having students see that the base does not always have to be the horizontal side is important.

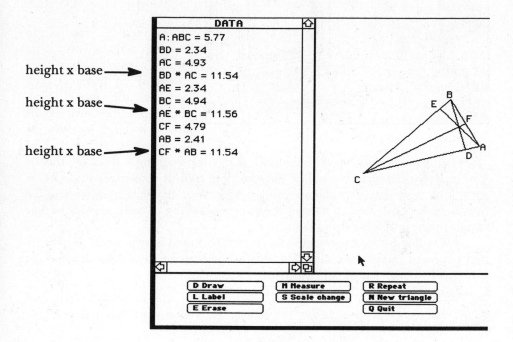

Teacher Response: _____

1. *Geometer's Sketchpad* (Key Curriculum Press) is available for both MS-DOS and Macintosh computers.

Up Front

BUSINESS NOT AS USUAL

I decided I wanted to create an activity that would review the basic ideas of my business class yet at the same time develop higher order skills like working backwards, looking for patterns, and connecting ideas and topics. I thought Wings for learning's *What Do You Do With a Broken Calculator?* would be just the right tool. It challenges students, as they solve a variety of problems using a calculator that has number and/or operation keys disabled, to deepen their understanding of basic operations and expand their problem solving skills.

With the overhead projector set up, I distributed a worksheet on which I had prepared an applied example of one of the mathematical formulas that my students had been studying in our text.

Equal rates as proportion: 300 words in 5 minutes. How many in 3?

$$\frac{300 \text{ words}}{5 \text{ minutes}} = \frac{n \text{ words}}{3 \text{ minutes}}$$

$$\frac{300}{5} = \frac{n}{3}$$

$$300 \times 3 = 5n$$

$$\frac{300 \times 3}{5} = n$$

$$\frac{900}{5} = 180 = n$$

Once they had properly set up the solution, I introduced the software program, using a TV monitor connected to my Apple IIe. I explained that the program enables them to use a calculator but with an unusual catch. I opened up *What Do You Do With A Broken Calculator?* and demonstrated: I entered the problem into the goal box and pointed out how the division key was disabled.

Soon I had the students brainstorming ideas for how to get around the difficulty of dividing by five when the division key won't work. We chose to try multiplying by its reciprocal 1/5, that is by its equivalent .20.

Then I asked for ideas to cope if the "3" key had also been disabled? The kids quickly got into the challenge. Using mental math and estimation skills, they were eager to propose strategies. They were putting their math skills to work without a second thought! And they were enjoying the problem-solving.

As students offered other solutions to the 3 key disability problem, I decided to set the criteria of using as few steps as possible as an additional goal. I had students individually write down the specific steps for implementing their strategies to the problem, when both the 3 key and the division key were disabled. After a few minutes, I invited solutions with the fewest steps and we tried them, watching the results on the projected monitor.

Then I divided the class into small teams of four students. I assigned each team five problems from the chapter review section of the textbook. Each team's task was to make the problems more interesting for solving on a calculator by specifying for each problem two disabled keys. The two keys could be any combination of digit or operation keys. In making up their problems, they were to list the disabled key for each problem on one sheet of paper, and what they felt was the strategy with the fewest steps for solving it on another. Later, the teams would solve one another's problems. And the team that succeeded in solving the most problems in the fewest steps would win.

The kids were tough in trying to create challenging problems for each other. It wasn't long before they wanted to disable 3 and 4 keys.

Teacher Tips:

1. Based upon the success of this lesson, I started to explore other features of What Do You Do With a Broken Calculator? The Problems activity card that comes with the product will generate problems dealing with place value, pattern of digits, alternative modes of operation, and/or estimation skills.

2. Another nice option is to use the "leading digit" calculator which permits the user to enter numbers with one significant digit. This is the ultimate challenge to alternative computation and mastery with numbers and algorithms. I found I was beginning to see possibilities for my prealgebra class, too.

The Kids' Perspective

COLLECTING SHAPES

Last fall we were supposed to learn about statistics. We talked about data averages, medians, and other boring stuff like that. It was almost Halloween and most of us were planning to "trick or treat," at least one more time. It just so happened Mr. Read decided to introduce computers to us at that time, with a "Halloween data" assignment. I have to admit, it was great. Who ever heard of doing homework by going out for Halloween? The only trick in Mr. Read's treat was that before we could eat any of our candy or stuff, we had to make an accounting of it by shape.

Names	Circle	Square	Rect.
Dan	3	3	7
Sharon	4	5	4
Ryan	1	8	7
Kristen	5	2	4
Beth	3	4	6
Matt	8	6	2
Robin	1	1	9
Pedro	6	8	2
Kim	3	6	8
Martin	9	7	9
Lindsey	5	4	6
Steve	3	7	4
Micheal	2	8	4
José	1	9	5
Maria	4	6	5
Jason	7	2	3
Jessica	5	4	6
Total	70	90	91

Well, he got us all involved in the process by helping to decide the day before to use these five shapes: circle, square, oval, rectangular, and other. We would bring our accountings back to class to put on the computer. We all made ourselves tally sheets with the names of every shape we had agreed on, so that everyone would count shapes the same way.

The next day we took turns entering our numbers in the spreadsheet on the computer and watched them add up. Before we could use the computer, each of us had to add up the information on our own tally sheets.

Oval	Other	Total
9	6	28
7	7	27
2	3	21
5	6	22
7	2	22
8	8	32
4	5	20
6	6	28
7	7	31
8	3	36
2	4	21
1	5	20
2	6	22
4	5	24
5	8	28
3	2	17
7	9	31
87	92	

We made guesses about what the whole classes final results would be. How many pieces of candy were collected in all? What was the most common shape? How big a percentage of the total did it represent? Did everybody have the same per-

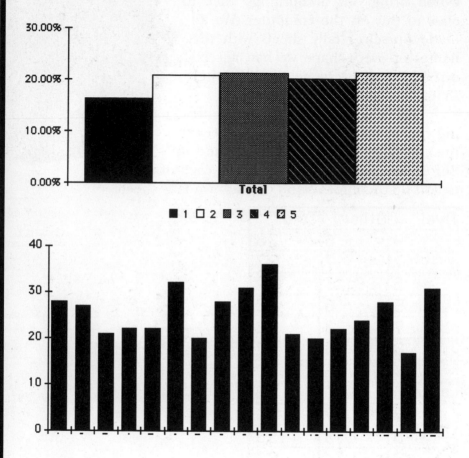

centage? In a big class discussion, we made a list of lots of things we wanted to know from the data, and then we asked the computer to show us the answers. Mr. Reed showed us how to make up these formulas to tell the program how to get answers for us.

We used *AppleWorks* spreadsheet software, but he said there are lots of spreadsheet programs that we could use if we wanted to do anything like this at home.

I really learned so much that day. As we all watched the numbers on the overhead screen, Mr. Read showed us how to select data for analysis. After seeing both the graphs and numbers, I began to understand better. Just talking numbers never made much sense to me, but seeing both the numbers and the graphs in columns standing next to each other helped me "get it" in a way that I really just hadn't been able to before.

Teacher Response:

Spreadsheet programs exist for all computers, and there are entire books about using spreadsheets in secondary math classes. I prefer to work with the simpler ones, like *MindPlay Works*, rather than the more complex business tools.

Up Front

BUDGET DEFICIT

After teaching junior high school math for fifteen years, I felt that the drab routine of my classes was beginning to get to me. It was time for a change. At the back of my classroom, a seldom used classroom computer seemed to beckon me. Maybe I could press it into action.

After investigating various possibilities, I decided to try a spreadsheet program. I figured that the spreadsheet might help my kids "think numbers," by giving them the chance to "manipulate" numbers to solve problems. And they could get instant feedback from the spreadsheet program.

So, what should the focus of the problems be? I racked my brain. Everyone was talking about group projects, but I didn't have much experience working with groups. Based on advice from friends and colleagues, however, I decided to do a group project on budgets. Since it was an election year, I chose the Federal budget. In a nut shell, my students would take turns working in "budget committee" groups to explore ways of reducing or increasing aspects of the budget according to requirements that I would specify.

From the World Almanac, I got the previous year's budget numbers. By working on separate line items, the students would have many possible solutions to problems. Variety would make the group work even more vital. I began to get excited. There were so many possibilities for the students to explore. I wondered, for instance, how they would respond if I specified that they had to reduce the budget by a number like one billion and they had to find a percentage by which all expenses must be reduced? How would they do if I gave them a total budget number and they would have to find the percentage it represented of the previous budget?

My first task was to introduce the spreadsheet and use of the computer. Using the software, I created a basic spreadsheet for them to work in. Using the LCD panel and overhead, I showed the kids how a spreadsheet was constructed with rows and columns. I was pleased to find that a few kids already had a "sense" for getting around in the program. Everyone noticed the blank column for indicating a percentage and the blank column that would show newly calculated amounts. At the bottom of that column, I inserted a formula for the new total budget.

Changing a line item meant entering a percentage in the appropriate empty cell in the percentage column. I demonstrated how by filling all the empty cells with decimals, one creates a completely new budget. This worked by entering a decimal and the computer calculated the new amount. Anything over 1.0 increased the number; any number less than 1 decreased the amount. As we entered each percentage, I had students predict the result before I pressed return. When the program instantly calculated each answer, they enjoyed seeing how well they had predicted.

When we were ready for the actual project, I created my "budget committees," making sure each group represented the spectrum of abilities in my class. With budget information in hand, the kids were to work together in their small groups to accomplish the following tasks:

- Reduce the total by $100,000,000 by changing each line item of expenses.
- Decrease the total budget by 10%, but simultaneously increase half of the expense line items.
- Increase revenues by a total of 12%, and decrease expenses to show a net gain of $80,000,000.

The kids frantically worked through the assignments. They scrambled to get time for their committee at the computer. Initially, I found I had to act as computer advisor during most of the class. I had hoped to be moving among the groups more to observe their planning for their budget work.

Nevertheless, the groups eventually did quite well. Despite my careful planning, I did have to "tweak" the classroom activity on the fly as I addressed unanticipated situations. Then things went well. Interestingly, most of the students said afterwards that they really didn't understand the numbers until they saw them using the computer spreadsheets.

Teacher Tips:

1. This one computer lesson worked quite well once everything was in sync. Be sure to have a spreadsheet template that's been tested and works. Also have a back up of the original.

2. If the class is inexperienced with this kind of activity, have a trained student as a computer assistant. Without this, the teacher will end up doing it, and unfortunately, not be helping other groups.

3. Even small group work requires that group members execute specific roles. Among the critical ones are computer operator, spokesperson, and recorder of information. Arrange groups accordingly.

Lesson Plan

RESEARCH IN MATHEMATICS

Grade Level: 7-9
Time Required: 1-2 class periods

Lesson Overview
Students will create a public opinion poll, then conduct it, and analyze and report the results.

Where It Fits in the Curriculum
Problem solving, measurement, statistics, sampling, percentages, probability, computational review, critical thinking.

Materials
One to three (or more) computers, any spreadsheet software (*AppleWorks*, *Microsoft Works*, etc.)

Skills Students Will Develop
Problem solving, statistical research, basic computation, data gathering.

Preparation
Review use of the spreadsheet program. Students should be able to create a simple table. Some students will need to be able to use spreadsheet functions like SUM, Standard Deviation, and graphing. Students should also have reviewed surveys, sampling, and questionnaire creation techniques (available in many text books).

Grouping and Roles
Three groups (or more, if you have more computers). Each group should have at least one student who has the computer spreadsheet skills mentioned above. If you have fewer than three computers available, groups can do the computer activity sequentially rather than simultaneously.

Procedures and Activities
❶ With the whole class, take 5-10 minutes to discuss the purposes of polling and ideas for polling research. Then assign groups and have each group create a five-question survey on a topic of their choice (e.g., students' awareness of the causes of AIDS). Before they break into small groups, go over each task in the Research Checklist.

Research Checklist

What is the main research question or hypothesis?
What is the universe from which the data will be selected?
How will you select your data sample?
How will you analyze the data on the computer?
What are your five questions?

■ ■ ■ ■ ■ ■ ■ ■ ■ ■ ■ ■ ■ ■ ■ ■

❷ Allow about 15-20 minutes for the groups to select their research area, develop their five questions designed to elicit the results, and create a mock up of the data spreadsheet they will use to manage the data they collect. Give groups a time limit that pressures them a bit and keeps them aware of time remaining. Often groups get down to serious work only minutes before deadlines.

❸ Have groups report their research plans to the entire class. Allow for questions and discussions after each report. This stage should take about 15- 20 minutes. Then give the groups 5-10 minutes to make a final revision of their plans.

❹ Execute the survey as homework (in lunch or homeroom periods, etc.).

❺ When the surveys are completed, the groups should enter the data on the classroom computer. Selection of graphs and other statistics is performed now. This stage should take about 10 minutes per group.

❻ As each group reports its results, focus discussion on evaluation of judgments. The specifics of the research plan are less important, except as they taint the resulting data. This stage should take 20 to 30 minutes.

Follow-up Activities/Extensions
- Invite other schools to replicate the research. Use telecommunications to see if results vary geographically.
- Analyze the data in greater depth. Use more sophisticated statistical tools to analyze the results.

The Kids' Perspective

CONSTRUCTING SOLUTIONS

The truth is I never really understood area, perimeter, and all that stuff. In fact, nobody in my seventh grade math class understood much. Fact is, we're what they call the "slow" group. But somehow, we got lucky, because we got a new teacher, Mr. Washington, and he brought a computer along with him, a Macintosh. Then things began to change. When he showed us this drawing program called *Aldus Superpaint,* I sat up and took notice. He dared us to try to fill up a big grid with movable blocks.

The computer drawing program made it easy to "mess around" and figure out the answers. He had us tell him what to do. We started by trying to fill the screen using a computer "block" that was 4 x 8, I think. We could move the block any way we wanted, but we had to come as close as we could to filling the space in. He called on kids to give him instructions. It took a while to figure out that we needed 30 4 x 8 blocks to fill this 24 x 40 grid.

After we finished, Mr. Washington showed us another way. He multiplied the grid edges 24 and 40 together to get the number 960 then he did the same with the little boxes and got 32. Then he divided. I learned that the number 960 divided by 32 is 30–the same as when we did the blocks.

The light dawned for me (and other kids, too). We were doing multiplication and division, but we did it with boxes and spaces that we could see and move. Now we decided to get some stuff from the math books that we really never understood, and tried to see if we could make grids to "play" with the numbers and learn this stuff.

What a neat class that was. I still remember it as a day when I began to feel that maybe I wasn't really as stupid as my teachers had made me feel before.

Teacher Response: _____

Superpaint, a fairly sophisticated paint program, is available from Aldus on the Macintosh. Many other simple paint programs at different levels of difficulty (*Paint Shop* from ComputerEasy, *Platinum Paint* from Beagle Brothers, *Dazzle Draw* from Broderbund) exist for other computers.

Up Front

TRY IT WITH TRIANGLES

While I've seen how students over the years could use SAS, SSS, etc. to prove triangles congruent, my intuition told me that my students really did not appreciate what conditions were necessary to determine a unique triangle. As teachers, we've been encouraged to provide opportunities for students to make observations and think inductively/intuitively through experimentation, yet for all practical purposes it seemed too time consuming. But I'm beginning to think that with the advent of computer drawing tools, such as the *GeoExplorer*, maybe we can incorporate more inductive-based lessons into the curriculum.

I introduced this material to my tenth-graders with the following problem:

> A building contractor has just assembled two triangular trusses that will support the roof in a community center. We already know that two triangles that are congruent have six corresponding parts that are congruent. Must the contractor check that all six corresponding parts are congruent or can he take a shortcut?

After I demonstrated how to use the toolbox of the *GeoExplorer*, the students used the software in cooperative groups of three, rotating the jobs of computer operator, recorder/spokesperson, and materials manager. I was hoping that the software program would eliminate the handicap and the anxiety of students who were not particularly adept with a compass and protractor/ruler.

The materials manager of each group received a worksheet that I had prepared instructing them to draw various triangles satisfying the given conditions (SS, AA, SA, SSS, AAA, SAS, SSA, AAS, ASA), collect measures, print nine copies of their computer workscreen, and state their conjectures.

Draw three triangles with the given information. Are they all the same size & same shape?

SS condition: AB = 8, BC = 5.
Sketch your triangles.

As I circulated among the working groups, I was pleased to hear some students suggest to one another that they try more examples in case the ones they had were special somehow. This suggestion showed that they were beginning to acquire an understanding of inductive reasoning.

When the students felt confident that they could defend their conclusions, the groups signed off on their worksheets and the materials managers of adjacent groups swapped worksheets. The groups then entered new values to see if they could verify the conclusions proposed on the worksheet given them. Once a conclusion survived two rounds, the materials manager could distribute its worksheet to all the groups.

After about twenty minutes of this process, I asked the class, "So what about the contractor?" The students were eager to return to the problem of the contractor and decide upon the best strategy. With all the information gathered, students wrote up their own theorems about proving triangles congruent and why they selected a particular method for the contractor. The recorder/spokes people, consolidated the writeups of all three members of their groups, submitted the final report to their groups for revision, then entered them with our word processing program. I printed the file containing all the group's reports and made copies for all the students.

As a class, we discussed the various reports and adopted the best solutions. The students were surprised to find that more than one solution qualified.

"Do you really think a contractor would make such a shortcut?" Karl asked. Laura and Mark simultaneously cried out, "So let's invite one to out class!"

Teacher Tips:

1. *GeoExplorer* is published by Scott Foresman and Company and is available for MS-DOS and Macintosh computers.

REFERENCES

1. <u>Author</u>: Larry Cuban
    <u>Title, Publisher, Date</u>: *Teachers and Machines: The Classroom Use of Technology Since 1920*. Teachers College Press, 1986.
    <u>Strengths</u>: Provides solid historical background on the very real difficulties and barriers to introducing new technologies to classroom teachers, in a way that can help practitioners acknowledge and empathize with the very real resistance many teachers have to computers.
    <u>Drawbacks</u>: Assumes perhaps too broadly that teacher resistance to technology is built in to the systems of schools as they now exist, rather than a response to the unthinking ways in which technology is usually introduced to classroom practitioners.

2. <u>Authors</u>: Tom Snyder and Jane Palmer
    <u>Title, Publisher, Date</u>: *In Search of the Most Amazing Thing: Children, Education, and Computers..* Addison Wesley, 1986.
    <u>Strengths</u>: Enthusiastic presentation of the potential of classroom computers beyond the usual CAI, drill and practice boundaries. Includes a useful description of the skills kids gain when using computer games and simulations. Acknowledges the "meager achievements" of school computers so far.
    <u>Drawbacks</u>: Some of the issues it discusses are now out of date.

3. <u>Author</u>: Anderson, Mary
    <u>Title, Publisher, Date</u>: *Partnerships: Developing Teamwork at the Computer* (Majo Press, 1988), 148 pp.
    <u>Strengths</u>: Provides teachers with good practical advice about ways to get maximum results from the combination of computers and cooperative learning.
    <u>Drawbacks</u>: The software it discusses is getting rapidly out-of date; some of it is very drill-and-practicy.

4. <u>Author</u>: David Docterman
    <u>Title, Publisher, Date</u>: *Great Teaching in the One Computer Classroom*. Tom Snyder Productions, 1988.
    <u>Strengths</u>: Provides good clear ideas about how to get the most out of a single classroom computer, for introducing new topics, stimulating lively student discussions, etc., and thus can help teachers re-conceptualize the uses of one computer within the classroom. Friendly style, big print, lively illustrations.

Drawbacks: The book shills shamelessly for Snyder software, neglecting the opportunity to illustrate how the value of lots of other great software could be maximized in the one computer classroom.

5. Author: William J. Masalski
   Title, Publisher, Date: *How to Use the Spreadsheet as a Tool in the Secondary School Mathematics Classroom*. NCTM, 1990.
   Strengths: Shows how the use of spreadsheets can free students from laborious manipulations of numbers, allowing them to concentrate on the mathematical problem itself; comes with two (Apple II) diskettes.
   Drawbacks: Requires either *Appleworks* or *Better Working Spreadsheet*.

6. Author: Daniel Chazen and Richard Houde
   Title, Publisher, Date: *How to Use Conjecturing and Microcomputers to Teach Geometry*. NCTM, 1989.
   Strengths: Shows how the use of computers can help teach students to behave like working mathematicians, conjecturing and proving geometrical concepts and ideas, through the use of the *Geometric Supposer* software series (WINGS).
   Drawbacks: Requires *Supposer* software.

7. Author: John C. Russell
   Title, Publisher, Date: *Spreadsheet Activities in Middle School Mathematics*. NCTM, 1992.
   Strengths: Shows how to provide a numerical problem solving tool to students for a variety of purposes (probability, proportion solvers, expanded notation, etc.).
   Drawbacks: Requires *Better Working Spreadsheet* (Apple only).

8. Author: North Carolina School of Science and Mathematics
   Title, Publisher, Date: *Matrices (Materials and software)*. NCTM, 1988.
   Strengths: Demonstrates the uses of matrices as models of real-world phenomena and as discrete data structures
   Drawbacks: Disk only available for IBM and compatibles.

9.. Author: J. Flake
   Title, Publisher, Date: *Computer-Intensive Middle and Secondary Mathematics Education*, Wadsworth Publishing, 1990
   Strengths: Focus on using technology intensively, rather than as adjunct or afterthought.
   Drawbacks: Not always as constructivist in approach as some citations above, and a little too general for immediate usage of some ideas.

10. <u>Author</u>: W.J.A. Mann and David Tall
    <u>Title, Publisher, Date</u>: *Computers in the Mathematics Curriculum.* (The Mathematical Association (259 London Rd., Leicester LE2 3BE, England), 1992.
    <u>Strengths</u>: Focuses on how students can be engaged to engage naturally in mathematics activity and offer opportunities for enhancing mathematics learning.
    <u>Drawbacks</u>: Emphasis on programming languages (BASIC, LOGO), not geared directly to NCTM standards and U.S. school divisions (primary, secondary, and "post-16").

11. <u>Author</u>: Rosamund Sutherland *et al.*
    <u>Title, Publisher, Date</u>: Spring, 1993 Feature Issue of *MicroMath*, on Algebra. Includes Sutherland's article on "Symbolising Through Spreadsheets," (20-22).
    <u>Strengths</u>: Focus on how the teaching of Algebra can be affected by both the computer and the calculator.
    <u>Drawbacks</u>: Some articles more relevant to issues in British schools.

12. <u>Author</u>: Eileen K. Schoaff
    <u>Title, Publisher, Date</u>: "How To Develop a Mathematics Lesson Using Technology," *Jl. of Computers in Mathematics and Science Teaching*, v.12, #1, 1993, 19-27.
    <u>Strengths</u>: Focus on using technology so that students are able to construct their own knowledge of mathematical concepts.
    <u>Drawbacks</u>: Though good overview, a little too general for immediate usage of ideas.

13. <u>Author</u>: John C. Whitmer
    <u>Title, Publisher, Date</u>: *Spreadsheets in Mathematics and Science Teaching.* School Science and Mathematics Association, Bowling Green State University, 1991.
    <u>Strengths</u>: Case studies to aid in the use of spreadsheets in twenty-one topic areas (probability, linear regression) at secondary level. Permission for copying all activities.
    <u>Drawbacks</u>: Not always as constructivist in approach as some citations above.

SOFTWARE LIST

This list includes all the software mentioned in this book. Each listing includes the title of the software and its publisher. If the software is readily available through a discount distributor, we have included the name of one such distributor and it's 800 telephone number. Otherwise, we have included the publisher's telephone number. Call the publisher or the distributor to get current information on pricing and machine platform availability.

Alge-Blaster
Davidson & Associates
Educational Resources (800-624-2926)

Algebra Concepts
Ventura Educational Systems
Learning Services (800-877-9378)

Algebraic Xpresser
William K. Bradford (800-421-2009)

AppleWorks
Claris
Educational Resources (800-624-2926)

Connectany
William K. Bradford (800-421-2009)

Dazzle Draw
Brøderbund
Educational Resources (800-624-2926)

Elastic Lines
Sunburst/WINGS for learning
(800-321-7511)

Excel
Microsoft (800-426-9400)

The Factory
Sunburst/WINGS for learning
(800-321-7511)

GeoExplorer
Scott Foresman (800-435-6621)

Geometer's Sketchpad
Key Curriculum Press (800-338-7638)

Geometric Presupposer
Sunburst/WINGS for learning
(800-321-7511)

Geometric Supposer
Sunburst/WINGS for learning
(800-321-7511)

Geometry Inventor
Sunburst/WINGS for learning
(800-321-7511)

GraphWiz
William K. Bradford (800-421-2009)

Green Globs (Part of *Graphing Equations*)
Sunburst/WINGS for learning
(800-321-7511)

Hands-on Math
Ventura Educational Systems
Learning Services (800-877-9378)

MathCAD
MathSoft, Inc. (800-628-4223)

Math Connections: Algebra 1
Sunburst/WINGS for learning
(800-321-7511)

Math Exploration Toolkit
IBM /EduQUEST (800-793-5327)

Microsoft Works
MicroSoft Corporation
Educational Resources (800-624-2926)

MindPlay Works
MindPlay (800-221-7911)

Ozone Depletion Module
William K. Bradford (800-421-2009)

Paint Shop
ComputerEasy
Educational Resources (800-624-2926)

Platinum Paint
Beagle Brothers
Educational Resources (800-624-2926)

Probability Theory
True Basic (800-872-2742)

Sim City
Maxis
Educational Resources (800-624-2926)

Statistics Workshop
Sunburst/WINGS for learning
(800-321-7511)

Superfactory
Sunburst/WINGS for learning
(800-321-7511)

Superpaint
Aldus
Educational Resources (800-624-2926)

3D Images
William K. Bradford (800-421-2009)

Voyage of the Mimi
Sunburst/WINGS for learning
(800-321-7511)

What Do You Do With a Broken Calculator?
Sunburst/WINGS for learning
(800-321-7511)

GETTING STARTED

Necessary Hardware/IBM

The program disk runs on the IBM PC, XT, or AT and many IBM compatibles with at least one disk drive and a minimum of 640 K of available RAM. The program runs under DOS 3.3 or later.

A printer is optional. The printers supported by the program are:

> all Epson printers and compatibles
> all IBM/ProPrinter printers and compatibles
> HP LaserJet and all compatibles

Your work is saved on a separate data disk or hard drive (with the extension .WRI).

Hard Drive Installation/IBM

If you have a hard drive you may install the program on it and run the program from there, while saving your work on floppies. Boot your machine the way you would normally. After the machine has booted, put the program disk into your floppy drive but do not change drives. From the hard drive prompt (C:>) type:

> A: install A C

To start the program, change directories to LESSPLAN and type **GO** at the prompt.

Floppy Drive Use/IBM

If your machine has two floppy drives and no hard drive, use the A: drive for the program disk, and the B: drive for your data disk. From the A> prompt type **GO**.

Necessary Hardware Macintosh

The program disk runs on the Macintosh with a minimum of 1 megabyte of available RAM. A printer is optional. Insert the program disk. (You may copy its contents onto the hard drive.) Click the program icon.

How to Begin

To begin work, you must first open a file. You can select New File from the File pull-down menu or select Open File if a file is available in the directory that you want to use.

Once you have a file open, you can enter and edit text in it. You can save your writing at any time. You can name and close the file and then open any other file that you previously made.

HOW TO USE THE WORD PROCESSOR

Take a few moments to familiarize yourself with the screen layout of the word processing program by opening a file in which to work. Notice the "menu bar" across the top of the screen.

Choosing from the Pull-down Menu Options

You select guide lessons and other program functions from the pull-down menus on the upper menu bar. Menu options that are grayed out are inactive. Shortcut keys are listed next to some menu options. Prompts for carrying out functions appear at the bottom of the screen (MS-DOS version).

MS-DOS MENUS

Help Menu

About Program gives information about the publisher and developer of the program.

Help (<F1>) is available from any part of the word processing program. When you access a Help Screen, you are really looking at one page in the Help Book. Use <PgUp/PgDn> to move back and forth in the Help Book.

Screen Display (Alt-S) allows you to customize the screen colors. Use the arrow keys to choose what you want changed and the <+> and <-> keys to change colors.

Data Path (Alt-D) allows you to change where the program will look for the data disk, referred to as the "default" data drive. Ordinarily this will be drive C. It displays the current drive and prompts you to enter the letter of the drive and the path where you want your work saved.

You cannot change drives while a file is open.

File Menu

The File Menu enables you to end your work in a file, as well as do other things such as printing and saving your files.

New File (<F8>) begins a new file. Enter a file name (up to 8 characters). Then begin work.

Open File (<F4>) opens any file that was created with this software and saved on your data disk. To open a file, select *Open File* (when no file is open), highlight a file name from the list that appears, and press <Enter>.

Close File (<F9>) closes a file when you want to stop working on it. To save changes you have made to a file without replacing the original file, choose *Save File;* then when you are asked if you want to use the same name, press N for No, and type in a new name for the file into the prompt area; then press <Enter>.

Insert File (<F7>) puts a file that has been made with this software into your open file. Put the cursor where the file is to be inserted, select *Insert File*, and in the prompt area enter the name of the file you want to insert.

Save File (<F3>) saves an open file in its present version and allows you to continue working on it.

Save as ASCII saves a copy of the open file in ASCII format. When a file is saved as an ASCII file, the program can not open it. The file is stripped of all special formatting. This is useful if you want to use a copy of your work with a different word processing program that can open ASCII files. The ASCII files have a file name extension of .ASC.

Print Options (<F6>) sets the printing options. Default values shown in the right-hand column below. They may be changed, within the limits in parentheses in the middle column. The program does not allow you to use numbers outside those limits. Options remain as set until you change them again or until you reload the program.

Title	FILENAME	
Left Margin	(1 - 65)	7
Right Margin	(10 - 79)	75
Line Spacing	(1 - 3)	1
Top Line	(1 - 60)	7
Bottom Line	(7 - 90)	60
Paper Length	(6 - 90)	66
Stop between Pages	(Y or N)	N
Page Numbering	(Y or N)	Y
Laser Printer	(Y or N)	N

Change "Stop between Pages" to Y for Yes if you intend to feed paper by hand. If the line spacing does not come out as you expected, check your printer manual for setup routines.

Print File (<F5>) prints the file you are working on using the Print Options as above or as you have set them. You may choose to print **All** the pages of your file or you may choose a **from** and **to** page range. Use the arrow keys to move the highlight.

Copy File duplicates a file that you choose from your data disk and puts the duplicate on the same data disk. To copy a file, select the file and type in the new file name for the copy; then press <Enter>.

Rename File enables you to give a new name to any file on your data disk. To rename a file, select the file and type in the new file name; then press <Enter>.

Erase File deletes files made with this program.

Quit closes the file you have open and quits the program.

Edit Menu

Undo (Alt-U) cancels the last Cut or Paste Text command. (You cannot undo other commands.) You can use the Undo function only immediately after you've cut or pasted text and before pressing any other keys.

Mark Text (Alt-M) allows you to mark a part of your document and then use Edit Menu and/or Format Menu functions on the marked text. Select Mark Text, then follow the instructions in the prompt area to highlight the text to mark. Then use <F2> to pull down a menu and select; or use the shortcut keys.

Cut Text (Alt-K) allows you to delete a marked part of your document. Select Cut Text after you have used Mark Text.

Copy Text (Alt-C) duplicates a part of your document. Select Copy Text after you have used Mark Text. The marked text is copied into the computer's memory until Alt-C or Alt-K is used again. Move the cursor to the place to insert the copy and Paste Text (see below).

Paste Text (Alt-P) pastes into your document a copy of text that you have marked and cut or copied. After you have used Cut or Copy Text, move the cursor to the place to insert the copy and select Paste Text. A copy of the text will appear in the new place.

Overstrike (<INS>) allows you to switch between Insert and Overstrike text entry mode. The bottom right corner of the screen indicates which text entry mode is active.

Find Menu

Find enables you to instruct the program to locate every occurrence of a "string" of characters. Choose *Find* from the Find Menu, then in the prompt area type in the "string," and then press <Enter>. *Find* starts at the cursor, loops through the end of the file and back to the cursor position until every instance of the string is found. Press <ESC> to cancel *Find.*

Replace replaces strings of characters. Choose *Replace* from the Find Menu, then type in the characters and spaces that you want to replace in the prompt area, then press <Enter>. Then type exactly what you want used instead and press <Enter>. (Although the *Find* function ignores upper and lower case, the replacement will use the upper and lower case characters exactly as you specify). Each time the string is found, the program asks if you want to replace it. <ESC> stops the *Replace* command but leaves all the changes already made.

Format Menu

Functions on the Format Menu determine how your work will appear on screen and in print.

Underline (Ctrl-U) Use this command immediately after you have used Mark Text (see above) to mark characters you want underlined. On the screen, the underlined text shows up as a different color.

Bold (Ctrl-B) Use this command immediately after you have used Mark Text (see above) to mark characters you want to appear in boldface. On the screen, the boldfaced text shows up as a different color.

Plain (Ctrl-P) Use this command immediately after you have used Mark Text (see above) to mark characters you want to appear in plain text. Plain removes Underline, Bold, Center, and Quote formatting.

Center (Ctrl-C) Use this command immediately after you have used Mark Text (see above) to mark characters you want to appear centered in your file. On the screen, everything will be centered until the next carriage return.

Quote (Ctrl-Q) Use this command immediately after you have used Mark Text (see above) to mark characters that are direct quotations and that you want to appear in your file indented and single spaced on the printed page. On the screen, any blocks of text formatted by Quote will be indented and single spaced.

Adjust Margins (Ctrl-J) Use this command immediately after you have used Mark Text (see above) to mark characters that you want to give special margins. Margins set with Ctrl-J override the margins set with Print Options. Each time you use this command, you are asked to enter the Left and Right Indent that you want. The adjusted margins remain in effect until the program encounters a carriage return in your text.

Line Spacing (Ctrl-S) sets line spacing (1>, 2>, or 3>). Mark the text you want to have special Line Spacing and then select Line Spacing from the Format Menu. You are then asked to type 1 for single spacing, 2 for double spacing, or 3 for triple spacing.

The spacing remains as set until the next carriage return. This command is useful when you want to change the line spacing for part of a document.

New Page (Ctrl-N) starts a new page. An N is displayed in the left margin with a dotted line and the Page Number, and the cursor moves to the next line to show where the inserted page is.

Guide Menu

To do the guide lessons, choose one listed in the Guide Menu. Whenever you choose a guide lesson, the computer screen splits horizontally, with the guide lesson that you chose appearing in the bottom part of the screen. Your working area (text entry area) remains at the top. You can still write in the text area and use the pull-down menus and help functions.

Each guide contains a number of "pages" on instruction. The prompt area tells you where you are in the lesson (example, "Page 3 of 9") as well as the commands to go forward <Ctrl-G> and to go backward <Ctrl-T>.

When an guide lesson is open, you can switch back to the full screen to write by pressing <ESC>. If you re-select that guide lesson from the Guide Menu, the program remembers where you were and picks up right where you left off.

Exit Guide when you have finished with a guide lesson, or to switch back to the full screen for writing. To switch back and forth between two guide lessons when you have one displayed already, just select the other from the menu. It will appear in the Guide window at the bottom of the screen. When you re-select the previous guide lesson, it will pick up just where you left off.

Practice Menu

Making a selection from the Practice Menu copies text into the open file so you can use the word processor to edit it. Any changes that you make in your file do not change the text items on this menu.

Usually instructions in a guide lesson you have chosen from the Guide Menu will tell you when to use a practice file. Once you are familiar with them, you may want to select them to use on your own whenever you want.

Notes Menu

The Notes Menu opens a database file of "records." You may not type in your file while the Notes options are in use.

View opens the file for browsing. If a record is too large to fit in the area at the bottom of the screen, use the Up and Down <ARROWS> to scroll the record. To move from one record to the next use the <PgUp> and <PgDn> keys. Pressing <ESC> closes the file.

Edit opens the database file with your cursor in it to enable you to edit records. Use the <ARROWS> to move the cursor in the record. Whatever you type will be entered at the cursor. The total amount allowed in each file is as follows:

Materials	100
Objectives	120
Activity	715
Grade level	10
Topic or Skills	60
Class/Group/Pair Activity	16

The <INS> key toggles between insert and overstrike mode. <Delete> and <backspace> enable you to erase. To move from one record to the next use <PgUp> and <PgDn>. Pressing <ESC> closes the file. Your changes are kept in the computer's memory until you save the Notes file or exit the program. To add a blank record to the database use <Ctrl-R> from the Edit record screen.

Find lets you select specific records by finding those that have a common element that you ask the program to look for. Choose *Find* from the Notes Menu, then press <Enter>. Type into the appropriate field the characters that you want the program to search for. Press <Ctrl-X> when you want to begin the search. *Find* will make active only those records that contain characters to match what you typed in. When the search is completed, the status line at the bottom of the screen will tell you how many records are active. When *Find* is used again, it will search through only the active records. With each new search, you are working with successively smaller and smaller subsets of the database file, until you press <Ctrl-A> to return to all records for a brand new search.

Copy enables you to mark a part of a record and put it into your open file, where you may use the word processor to edit it. Use View or Find to display the record you want to copy from, then select *Copy* from the Notes Menu. The cursor will appear in the record. Follow the instructions in the prompt area to *Mark* and *Copy* what you want. The cursor will then appear in your writing file. Move it to the place where you want to insert the copy and press <Enter>.

Special Keys

Special function keys available in the word processing program.

<F1>	Help	<F6>	Print Options
<F2>	Menu	<F7>	Insert File
<F3>	Save File	<F8>	New File
<F4>	Open File	<F9>	Close File
<F5>	Print File	<F10>	Quit

Special short cut commands in the word processing program.

<Alt-U>	Undo
<Ctrl-U>	Underline
<Alt-M>	Mark Text
<Ctrl-B>	Boldface
<Alt-K>	Cut Text
<Ctrl-P>	Plain
<Alt-C>	Copy Text
<Ctrl-C>	Center
<Alt-P>	Paste Text
<Ctrl-Q>	Quote
<Alt-F>	Find
<Ctrl-J>	Adjust Margins
<Alt-R>	Replace
<Ctrl-S>	Line Spacing
<Alt-S>	Screen Display
<Ctrl-N>	New Page
<Alt-D>	Set Data Path

<ESC>	cancel a command, back out of a screen
<ARROWS>	move the cursor
<BACKSPACE>	erase backward (to the left of the cursor)
<DEL>	erase forward (erase the cursor character or space)
<INS>	change between INSERT and OVERSTRIKE

MACINTOSH MENUS

File Menu
(See section under MS-DOS Menus.)

Save as... renames the open file and saves it with a new name.

You may choose to save the file in Normal or Text File Format. The program can only open files saved in Normal File Format.

Page Setup... and **Page Margins...** determines how your document will be printed. See your printer manual for information regarding the Page Setup dialog box. Page Margins have been set for normal 8 1/2" by 11" page printing. You may change any or all of the four margins (top, bottom, left, and right). You may also set the starting page number.

Show by Page displays a small facsimile of your document.

Print... (⌘ P) enables you to print your work. For information about the options in the dialog box, refer to your printer manual.

Edit Menu
(See section under MS-DOS Menus. Note: Mark Text in standard Macintosh way, that is, click and drag.)

Clear deletes marked text.

Select All (⌘ A) marks your entire document. Whatever function you then choose will affect the entire contents.

Find/Replace (⌘ F) lets you find a string of characters or find and replace a string with another string.

Find Next (⌘ N) takes you to the next occurrence of the string you have specified.

Show/Hide Ruler and **Show/Hide ¶** are "toggles" that reveal information about the format of your page. Click *Show Ruler* if you want to display a ruler across the top of the screen. You can then see where the line length is set and where you have placed any Tabs. (Leaving it turned off gives you a little more on-screen space for writing.)

Font Menu

The Font Menu allows you to select any of the fonts for your documents.

Style Menu

This menu allows you to select type styles and sizes for what you write in the program.

Format Menu

Line Spacing allows you to change the default width of space between lines. Enter the spacing you want in the dialog box. To return to the default spacing, enter the number 0 in the dialog box. If you place the cursor at the beginning of a new line and then change the line spacing, the line spacing you specify will remain in effect as you enter text until you change it back.

Set Tab allows you to set your tabs. When you click this function, the ruler is displayed with a small pointer as your cursor. Use the mouse to put the pointer at the position on the ruler where you want to set the tab. Once a tab has been set, you can move it to other positions; use the mouse to activate the pointer and then drag it to its new location on the ruler. To delete it altogether, drag it into the writing area.

Align Left, **Align Right**, **Center**, and **Justify** options enable you to set the placement of text on the page. This function affects the entire paragraph where your cursor is. Normally text is left-justified (the default setting), which means it lines up along the left margin. If you want to change the placement of a paragraph, select the paragraph that you want changed by clicking in it; then select *Align Right*, *Center*, or *Justify* from the Format Menu. Highlighting text in more than one paragraph will cause the function to affect each paragraph.

Open Header and **Open Foote**r allow you to put page numbers (or other text) at the top and/or bottom of each page of your printed text. Click on either of these options and enter the text you want to have printed. The paragraph symbol indicates a carriage return has already been entered. Enter your text in front of that carriage return. You can enter additional carriage returns by pressing Return.

To have the printer number your pages, select *Insert Page Number* after you have chosen *Open Header* or *Open Footer*. If you want the page number centered, use the *Center* option on the Format Menu.

Guide Menu
(See section under MS-DOS Menus.)

If the guide lesson will not fit in the guide display area, the scroll bar to the right is active and "(scroll)" appears at the bottom of the window. Use the mouse to switch the active scroll bar between the guide area and the text entry area.

Practice Menu
(See section under MS-DOS Menus.)

Notes Menu
(See section under MS-DOS Menus.)

View\Edit (⌘ J) opens a database of notecard records. If a record is too large to fit in the area at the bottom of the screen, the scroll bar next to the record is available. To move from one notecard to the next, use the Next and Previous buttons in the prompt line or *Next Record* and *Previous Record* from the Notes Menu. Clicking the Exit button or selecting *Exit Notes* from the Notes Menu closes the database file.

To edit a notecard in the database, select *View\Edit* from the Notes Menu and move to the notecard you want to edit by clicking the Next or Previous buttons. Double-click below the "field name." The field expands to fill the bottom area and your cursor is active there. Whatever you type will be entered at the cursor. When you have finished editing any field and want to keep the changes, click the Done button. Click the Cancel button to exit the "Edit mode" without saving your work on the notecard.

Find Notes (⌘ K) opens a dialog box for you to type into the appropriate field the sequence of letters that you want the program to search for. Click the Begin Search button when you want to begin the search.

When the search is completed, a dialog box appears which tells you how many records are active. To return to all the records for a brand new search, click the All button or select *All Records* from the Notes Menu.

Copy Notes (⌘ L) allows you to copy text from all fields of a record and paste it into your file. First, display the record that you want to copy from. Then select *Copy Notes*. The cursor will appear in the record. Use the mouse to highlight the part of the notecard that you want. Then select *Copy* from the Edit Menu. Put your cursor into your writing file where you want the notecard; then select *Paste* from the Edit Menu. The database file remains in "Copy Notes mode" until you click the Next or Previous button.

If you have edited the notecard presently displayed, a dialog box will appear and ask if you want to save. Click the Yes button to save the current version of the notecard.

Next Record (⌘])/**Previous Record** (⌘ [ ) moves through the Notes database one record at a time.

Add Record (⌘ D) adds an empty record to the end of the database. You may then enter text and edit the record using the "Edit mode" of *View/Edit*.

All Records undoes any Find Notes searches and makes all the records active.

Exit Notes closes the Notes display area. If you have edited the notecard displayed, a dialog box will offer you the opportunity to save it. If there was a guide lesson open before the Notes option was used, that guide reappears.

Special Keys

Listed below are special function keys available in the word processing program. Menus show the shortcut keys.

(⌘ O)	Open...	(⌘ T)	Plain Text
(⌘ W)	Close	(⌘ B)	Bold
(⌘ S)	Save	(⌘ I)	Italics
(⌘ P)	Print...	(⌘ U)	Underline
(⌘ Q)	Quit	(⌘ G)	Next Page
(⌘ Z)	Undo	(⌘ R)	Previous Page
(⌘ X)	Cut	(⌘ E)	Exit Guide
(⌘ C)	Copy	(⌘ J)	View
(⌘ V)	Paste	(⌘ K)	Find Notes
(⌘ A)	Select All	(⌘ L)	Copy Notes
(⌘ F)	Find/Replace	(⌘])	Next Record
(⌘ N)	Find Next	(⌘ [ )	Previous Record
		(⌘ D)	Add Record

<ESC>	cancel a command, back out of a screen
<ARROWS>	move the cursor
<DELETE>	erase backward (to the left of the cursor)